Hampton-Brown
EDGE

NATIONAL GEOGRAPHIC LEARNING

CENGAGE Learning

Acknowledgments

Grateful acknowledgment is given to the authors, artists, photographers, museums, publishers, and agents for permission to reprint copyrighted material. Every effort has been made to secure the appropriate permission. If any omissions have been made or if corrections are required, please contact the Publisher.

Photographic Credits

Cover: Standing in Awe of the Aurora, Northwest Territories, Canada, Robert Postma. Photograph © Robert Postma/First Light/Getty Images.

For product information and technology assistance, contact us at
Customer & Sales Support, 888-915-3276

For permission to use material from this text or product, submit all requests online at **www.cengage.com/permissions**
Further permissions questions can be emailed to
permissionrequest@cengage.com

National Geographic Learning | Cengage Learning
1 Lower Ragsdale Drive
Building 1, Suite 200
Monterey, CA 93940

Cengage Learning is a leading provider of customized learning solutions with office locations around the globe, including Singapore, the United Kingdom, Australia, Mexico, Brazil, and Japan. Locate your local office at **www.cengage.com/global**.

Visit National Geographic Learning online at **ngl.cengage.com**
Visit our corporate website at **www.cengage.com**

Printed in the USA.
Sheridan, KY, A CJK Group Company

ISBN: 978-12857-34835 (Practice Book)
ISBN: 978-12857-34873 (Practice Book Teacher's Annotated Edition)

ISBN: 978-12857-66942 (Practice Masters)
Teachers are authorized to reproduce the practice masters in this book in limited quantity and solely for use in their own classrooms.

Printed in the United States of America

20 21 22 23 24

15 14

Contents

Contents, *continued*

UNIT 4

UNIT 5

Contents, *continued*

UNIT 7

Grammar: Complex Sentences

Grammar: Present Perfect Tense

Grammar: Fragments and Combination Sentences

② What Do You Need for a Sentence?

A Subject and a Predicate

A complete sentence has two parts: the **subject** and the **predicate**.

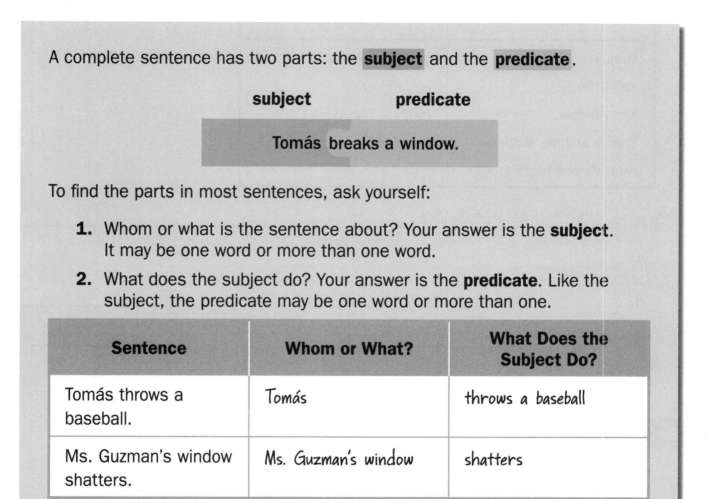

subject	predicate

Tomás breaks a window.

To find the parts in most sentences, ask yourself:

1. Whom or what is the sentence about? Your answer is the **subject**. It may be one word or more than one word.

2. What does the subject do? Your answer is the **predicate**. Like the subject, the predicate may be one word or more than one.

Sentence	Whom or What?	What Does the Subject Do?
Tomás throws a baseball.	Tomás	throws a baseball
Ms. Guzman's window shatters.	Ms. Guzman's window	shatters

Try It

A. Match each subject to a predicate.

1. The window   believes Tomás.

2. Glass   went too far.

3. Tomás   says it was an accident.

4. The ball   is broken.

5. Ms. Guzman   covers the ground.

B. Choose words from each column to make five sentences. Write the sentences on the lines.

Subject	Predicate
Tomás	become friends.
Ms. Guzman	are important.
The window	forgives Tomás.
Tomás and Ms. Guzman	gets fixed.
Honesty and forgiveness	says he's sorry.

6. _Tomás says he's sorry._ _____

7. _____

8. _____

9. _____

10. _____

Write It

C. Answer the questions. Add a predicate to each subject to tell what you think.

11. What does honesty mean to you? Honesty _____
_____.

12. What does forgiveness mean to you? Forgiveness _____
_____.

D. (13–15) Write at least three sentences that tell why it is important to apologize and to forgive. Remember to include a subject and a predicate in each sentence.

_____

_____

_____

_____

_____

3 What Is a Sentence About?
The Subject

The **complete subject** can be one word or a phrase of several words. The noun is the most important word in the subject. A **noun** is the name of a person, place, or thing.

1. This **shop** sells clothes.
2. **Workers** sew the clothes in factories.
3. Many of the **factories** are old.
4. **Conditions** are very poor.
5. The **shopkeeper** knows about this.

Nouns in the Subject	
Person	workers shopkeeper
Place	shop factories
Thing	conditions

Try It

A. Complete the subject of the sentence. Add a noun from the chart above.

1. The ___shopkeeper___ buys from factories.

2. The _____ are hot and crowded.

3. _____ are not well paid.

4. _____ are getting worse.

5. This _____ does not deserve our business!

B. Complete each subject. Add a noun from the box.

| family   people   sign   woman |

6. A tall ___woman___ carries a sign.

7. The _____ shows the workers' wages.

8. Many _____ protest the low wages.

9. My _____ won't shop at the store.

Write It

C. Answer each question with a sentence. Be sure your subject includes a noun.

10. Who deserves fair wages? All _____ deserve fair wages.

11. What should be clean and safe? All _____ should be clean and safe.

12. Who should be treated with respect? All _____

_____ .

D. (13–15) When you boycott someone or something, you refuse to deal with that person, place, or thing. Write at least three sentences telling about something that should be boycotted. Remember to include a noun in each subject.

_____

_____

_____

_____

_____

Edit It

E. (16–20) Edit the journal entry below. Fix five subjects.

May 15

My older sister joined a protest march today. The was held to make people aware of a new store. The sells sports shoes from another country. Many were paid low wages to make the shoes. The should be boycotted!
All should be paid fairly.

Proofreader's Marks

Add text:
                    wages
Their ^ are low.

See all Proofreader's Marks on page ix.

Name _____   Date _____

4 What's the Most Important Word in the Predicate?
The Verb

- The **complete predicate** in a sentence often tells what the subject does. It can be one word or several words. The **verb** shows the action.

  A new student **comes** to school.
  Some of my friends **ignore** him.

- Sometimes the predicate tells what the subject has. It uses these **verbs**:

  The new student **has** a great smile.
  My friends **have** no reason to dislike him.

- Other times, the predicate tells what the subject is or is like. The **verb** is a form of **be**.

  The new student **is** a friendly person.
  My friends **are** unkind to him.
  I **am** unhappy about this.

Try It

A. Complete each sentence with a verb. Add a verb from the box.

| ask   has   have   is   sits |

1. The new student _____ alone.

2. I _____ an idea.

3. I _____ the new student to join us.

4. The new student's name _____ Eric.

5. Eric _____ a good sense of humor.

B. Complete each sentence with a verb.

6. Eric _____ an older brother.

7. Eric and his brother _____ athletes.

8. My friends _____ to Eric's football stories.

9. Eric _____ the center of attention!

Write It

**C. A new student comes to your school. What do you do? Answer the questions.
Use a verb in each sentence.**

10. What do you say to your friends? I _____

_____.

11. How do you show you are a kind person? I _____

_____.

**D. (12–14) Now write at least three sentences to tell how you would make a new
student feel welcome at your school. Remember to use a verb in each predicate.**

_____

_____

_____

_____

Edit It

E. (15–20) Edit the letter below. Fix six predicates. Use the verbs has, have, is, are, and am.

Dear Granddad,

    I am happy at my new school. I some new friends. I sat with them at lunch. They easy to talk to. I told them about playing football. One boy friendlier than the others. He a brother, too. They both athletes, too. Please come visit soon! I so much to tell you.

Your grandson,

Eric

Proofreader's Marks
Add text:
Your brother ^is friendly.
See all Proofreader's Marks on page ix.

5 Write Complete Sentences

Remember: You need a **subject** and a **predicate** to make a complete sentence. Often, the most important word in the subject is a **noun**. Every predicate needs a **verb**.

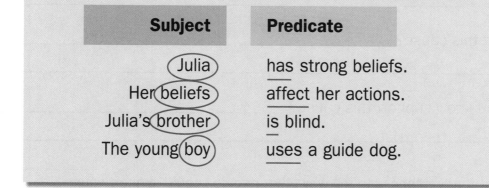

The **noun** is the most important word in the **subject**.
The **verb** is the most important word in the **predicate**.

Subject	Predicate
Julia	has strong beliefs.
Her beliefs	affect her actions.
Julia's brother	is blind.
The young boy	uses a guide dog.

Try It

A. Complete the subject or predicate to make a complete sentence.

1. Julia _____ a favorite cause.

2. _____ tells people about the importance of guide dogs.

3. Guide dog puppies _____ in foster homes.

4. Kind and patient _____ raise them.

5. The _____ just need the right care!

B. Draw a line from each subject to the correct predicate.

6. Julia's brother   is very well trained.

7. The dog   raised the dog as a puppy.

8. A foster family   has a guide dog.

9. Then a trainer   are partners.

10. The boy and the dog   worked with the dog.

C. Write sentences about a cause you support. Be sure each sentence has a subject and a predicate.

11. What cause do you support? I _____ the cause of_____.

12. Who or what is helped by this cause? _____

_____

13. Why do you support this cause? _____

_____

14. Do other people you know support this cause? _____

_____

D. (15–18) Now write at least four sentences to tell why other people should support your cause. Remember you need a subject and a predicate to make a complete sentence.

_____

_____

_____

_____

_____

Edit It

E. (19–25) Edit the article below. Fix seven mistakes.

Guide Dog Volunteers

Tanya Jackson raises guide dog puppies. The puppies in her home for 18 months. Then go to guide dog school. Tanya like a foster parent to the pups.

Tanya learned about this work from Julia Brown. Julia's has a guide dog. Now knows how important guide dogs are. She her own time. She people about guide dog programs.

Proofreader's Marks

Add text:
                         are
Guide dogs ^ helpful.

See all Proofreader's Marks on page ix.

⑥ What's a Plural Noun?

A Word That Names More Than One Thing

One	More Than One
A **singular noun** names one thing.	A **plural noun** names more than one thing.

Use these spelling rules for forming plural nouns.

1. To make most nouns plural, just add -**s**.

2. If the noun ends in **s**, **z**, **sh**, **ch**, or **x**, add -**es**.

3. If the noun ends in **y** after the consonant, change the **y** to **i** and add -**es**.

4. Some nouns have special plural forms.

One	More Than One
goal	goal**s**
hope	hope**s**
sketch	sketch**es**
destiny	destin**ies**
city	cit**ies**
man	men
tooth	teeth

Try It

A. (1–6) Complete the chart. Write the plural form of each noun.

Singular Nouns (one)	Plural Nouns (more than one)
career	careers
student	
desire	
loss	
penny	
man	

B. Complete each sentence. Write the plural of the noun in parentheses.

7. Most _____*people*_____ have goals, or things they want to achieve. **(person)**

8. Students want to get good _____. **(grade)**

9. Parents want the best for their _____. **(child)**

10. _____ want a happy home life. **(Family)**

11. Working men and _____ want rewarding careers. **(woman)**

12. We all have desires and _____. **(wish)**

13. Setting goals helps us lead better _____. **(life)**

Write It

C. Use at least one plural noun to write about your goals, wishes, and dreams.

14. Write about some of your goals in school this year. _____

_____

15. Write about one of your wishes. _____

_____

16. Write about one of your dreams for the future. _____

_____

D. (17–20) Write at least four sentences to tell why it is important to have goals in life. Use at least four plural nouns in your writing. Remember to use the correct form of plural nouns.

_____

_____

_____

_____

_____

⑦ How Do You Know What Verb to Use?

Match It to the Subject.

Forms of *Be*: am, is, are

I + am	I **am** on the team.
she + is	She **is** the team captain now.
he + is	He **is** a big fan.
it + is	It **is** time for elections.
we + are	We **are** excited to find a new captain.
you + are	You **are** a team member.
they + are	They **are** team members, too.

Try It

A. (1–6) Complete each sentence in the paragraph. Use **am**, **is**, or **are**.

I _____*am*_____ hopeful about the position of team captain. But I

_____ hesitant, too. Many of the players _____ indifferent.

We _____ in trouble as a team. You _____ aware of this. It

_____ time for a change.

B. Complete each sentence. Use the verb **am**, **is**, or **are**. Match the verb to the subject.

7. One player _____ disrespectful.

8. Other players _____ unconcerned.

9. The coach _____ interested in team players.

10. It _____ a difficult situation.

11. I _____ ready to take charge.

12. You _____ willing to help me.

C. Answer the questions. Use **am**, **is**, and **are** in your answers.

13. What is the role of a good team leader? The role _____

_____.

14. What are some challenges a team leader faces? Some challenges _____

_____.

15. What can a leader say to players to inspire them? A leader _____

_____.

D. (16–19) Pretend you are a team captain. Write at least four sentences that you would say to your team to help them reach their goals. Use **am**, **is**, and **are** in your sentences.

_____

_____

_____

_____

E. (20–25) Edit the letter. Fix six incorrect verbs. Make sure to use **am**, **is**, and **are** correctly.

Coach,
    I am happy to accept the role of team captain. The players am difficult. Some are even disrespectful. But the team are capable of great things. My co-captain and I are committed to working hard. You is a role model for us.
    It are time for a winning season. We ready to begin. I is anxious to get to work!
Brett

Proofreader's Marks

Change text:
                    is
Hard work am necessary.

See all Proofreader's Marks on page ix.

8 How Do You Know What Action Verb to Use?
Match It to the Subject.

- **Action verbs** tell when a subject does something, like **strum**, **tap**, or **wait**.
- Action verbs do not change form when the subject is **I** or **you**.

   1. I **strum** my guitar.   **2.** You **strum** your banjo.
   3. I **tap** my right foot.   **4.** You **tap** your left foot.
   5. I **wait** for you to join in.   **6.** You **wait** for me to begin.
   7. I **sing** the melody.   **8.** You **sing** harmony.

- Some sentences have more than one action verb. All the verbs must match the subject.
   I **hear** the song, **memorize** it, and **sing**.

Try It

A. Complete each sentence. Write the correct form of the verb.

1. I _____dream_____ of being in a band.
   dream / dreams

2. I _____ my guitar everywhere.
   carry / carries

3. You _____ in a popular band.
   play / plays

4. You _____ around the country.
   travel / travels

5. You _____ like a serious musician.
   look / looks

6. I _____ like a high-school student.
   dress / dresses

7. You _____ many listeners.
   attract / attracts

8. I _____ a new image for myself!
   want / wants

B. Complete each sentence with a verb from the box. Use each verb twice.

listen	practice	say	share	think

9. I _____ music is important.

10. You _____ a good education is important, too.

11. You _____ your music on the road.

12. I _____ my music at school.

13. I _____ ideas with my friends.

14. You _____ ideas with other musicians.

15. I _____ to music on the radio.

16. You _____ to live musicians.

17. I _____ that being a good musician is my goal.

18. You _____ that being a good musician is rewarding.

Write It

C. Imagine that you are talking to a friend who inspires you. Complete each sentence with two action verbs. Make sure the verbs match the subject.

19–20. I _____ and _____.

21–22. You _____ and _____.

D. (23–25) What else would you say to your friend about reaching your goals? Write at least three more sentences. Use **I** and **you** as the subjects. Make sure each verb matches the subject.

_____

_____

_____

_____

⑨ How Do You Know What Action Verb to Use?
Match It to the Subject.

- **Action verbs** tell when a subject does something.
- If the sentence is about one other person, place, or thing, add **-s** to the action verb.

   1. Marta **walks** down the hall.   **2.** Her friends **walk** down the hall, too.

   3. Marta **wears** a beautiful shirt.   **4.** Her friends **wear** baggy sweaters.

   5. Marta **pays** very little for clothes.   **6.** Many teens **pay** a lot for clothing.

   7. Marta **shows** her creativity.   **8.** Her friends **show** their admiration.

- Some sentences have more than one action verb. All the verbs must agree with the subject.

   Marta **looks** at clothing and **knows** what to buy.
   Her friends **watch** Marta and **learn** from her.

Try It

A. Complete each sentence. Write the correct form of the verb.

   1. Marta _____ to design clothes.

want / wants

   2. Marta _____ inexpensive shirts.

buy / buys

   3. She _____ her own embellishments.

add / adds

   4. Her shirts _____ a fashion expert.

attract / attracts

B. Write the correct form of the verb in parentheses.

   5. The woman _____ Marta's shirts. **(like)**

   6. Marta _____ flattered and inspired. **(feel)**

   7. Marta _____ other shirts. **(design)**

C. Answer these questions about a talented friend. Use the correct form of action verbs in your sentences.

8. What does your friend do? My talented friend _____

_____.

9. How do other people inspire your friend? Other people _____

_____.

D. (10–13) Now write about the talents you have. Who inspires you? Write at least four sentences. Remember to use the correct form of action verbs.

_____

_____

_____

_____

_____

Edit It

E. (14–20) Edit the article. Fix seven action verbs. Use the correct form.

A Talented Teenager

Marta Mendez attends Valley High School. She goes to class like all the other teenagers at school. She laugh and talks with friends in the hall. Yet Marta stand out in the crowd. What set Marta apart? Marta is a clothing designer. She make and wear designer shirts. Marta buy everyday shirts and change them into dazzling designs. Marta is a designing genius!

Proofreader's Marks

Change text:
makes
What make her special?

See all Proofreader's Marks on page ix.

10 Make Subjects and Verbs Agree

Remember: The verb you use depends on your subject.
These subjects and verbs go together.

Forms of *Be*
I **am** special.
You **are** special.
He, she, or it **is** special.
We, you, or they **are** special.

Action Verbs
I **need** my friends.
You **need** your family.
He, she, or it **needs** care.
We, you, or they **need** each other.

Try It

A. Complete each sentence. Write the correct form of the verb.

1. I _____ one of many siblings.
   am / are

2. We _____ members of a large family.
   is / are

3. My parents _____ hard to inspire us.
   work / works

4. I _____ to accomplish many things.
   plan / plans

5. My dad _____ pride in my accomplishments.
   show / shows

6. My mom _____ me she's proud, too.
   tell / tells

B. Complete each sentence with a verb from the box.

admire	is	marvel	try

7. I greatly _____ Uncle Jack.

8. I always _____ to follow his example.

9. Uncle Jack _____ my inspiration.

10. People _____ at his dedication and skill.

Write It

C. Answer the questions about yourself and people you admire. Be sure each verb agrees with the subject.

11. Whom do you admire? I _____ .

12. Why is this person an inspiration to you? _____

13. What talents do you have? _____

14. Whom do you want to inspire? _____

D. (15–18) Now write at least four sentences to tell more about people you admire and how they influence you. Remember to make subjects and verbs agree.

_____

_____

_____

_____

_____

Edit It

E. (19–25) Edit the journal entry. Fix seven mistakes. Be sure each verb agrees with the subject.

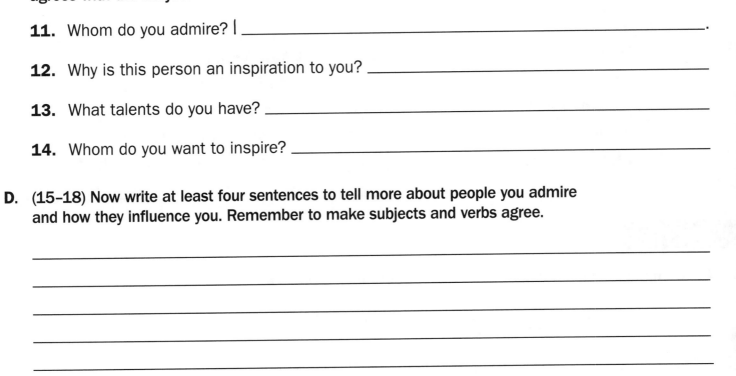

June 22

I always enjoy my visits with Uncle Jack. He tell me about his years as a baseball player. His old jersey and cap is in the attic. They reminds me of what Uncle Jack accomplished. He played for a major league team. He remain a part of baseball history today. People admires him. I wants to stand out like Uncle Jack. I is talented, too!

Proofreader's Marks

Change text:
They *are* is in great condition.

See all Proofreader's Marks on page ix.

11 What Is a Fragment?

It's an Incomplete Sentence.

A **fragment** is a group of words that begins with a capital letter and ends with a period. It looks like a sentence, but it is not complete. A subject or a verb may be missing.

Fragments	Sentences
1. Hears about a computer sale.	Marvin hears about a computer sale.
2. Are very cheap.	The computers are very cheap.
3. The deal good.	The deal sounds good.
4. Brings cash to the sale.	Marvin brings cash to the sale.

Try It

A. Write whether each group of words is a fragment or a sentence. If it is a fragment, change it to a sentence by adding a subject or a verb.

1. Marvin the computer home. _fragment; Marvin takes the computer home._

   _____

2. Doesn't work. _____

   _____

3. Marvin hears a news story about the computers. _____

   _____

4. Finds out that the computers were stolen. _____

   _____

5. The computer sellers have left town. _____

   _____

6. Committed a crime. _____

   _____

B. Underline the fragment. Then add a subject or a verb to the fragment. Write the new sentence on the line.

7. Many people believe scammers. They what they are told.

     _____

8. Scammers make money dishonestly. Often sell damaged goods.

     _____

9. Have you ever been fooled by a scammer? Should be careful.

     _____

10. Think carefully about deals that sound too good. Probably aren't!

     _____

Write It

C. What schemes or scams have you seen or heard of? Write complete sentences to tell about them.

11. I saw _____

     _____.

12. I heard of _____

     _____.

D. (13–15) Write at least three sentences to tell why you think people fall for schemes and scams. Include a subject and a verb in each complete sentence you write.

_____

_____

_____

_____

_____

12 What's One Way to Fix a Fragment?

Add a Subject.

- A complete sentence has a **subject** and a **predicate**.
- To check for a subject, ask yourself:
  Whom or what is the sentence about?

Fragments	Complete Sentences
1. Hears an exciting story.	Jenna hears an exciting story.
2. Wants to believe it.	She wants to believe it.
3. Is outlandish.	The story is outlandish.
4. Talk about it all day.	Students talk about it all day.

Try It

A. (1–7) Find seven fragments. Fix each fragment by adding a subject.

Jenna believes outlandish stories. Heard a story about a bear in a grocery store. Was growling in the aisles. Customers were scared. Screamed and ran out of the store. The bear was hungry. Chewed up pounds of cheese and meat. Wildlife officers trapped the bear. Took it back to the woods. Thinks the story is true. Tells her friends about it.

Proofreader's Marks

Do not capitalize:

The Story is outlandish.

Add text:
you
Can believe that?

See all Proofreader's Marks on page ix.

B. Fix each fragment by adding a subject. Write the complete sentence.

8. Wants to be popular. _____

9. Thinks telling stories will bring her attention. _____

_____

10. Are usually not true tales. _____

11. Told me a story about a bear in a grocery store. _____

_____

12. Did not believe the story. _____

13. Did not spread the story around. _____

Write It

C. Answer the questions. Write complete sentences. Be sure each sentence has a subject.

14. What is the topic of an outlandish story you have heard? The topic _____

_____.

15. Who told the story? _____

_____

16. Who believed the story? _____

_____

D. (17–20) Write at least four sentences to tell about a time you told an outlandish story or believed one. Remember to include a subject in each sentence.

_____

_____

_____

_____

_____

13 What's Another Way to Fix a Fragment?

Add a Predicate, and Be Sure It Has a Verb.

When you write a sentence, be sure to include the verb. If you leave the verb out, the words you write are a **fragment**.

Fragments	Complete Sentences
1. My parents honest people.	My parents are honest people.
2. They always the truth.	They always tell the truth.
3. I honesty, too.	I value honesty, too.
4. I my parents to trust me.	I want my parents to trust me.

Try It

A. (1–5) Find five fragments. Fix each fragment by adding a verb.

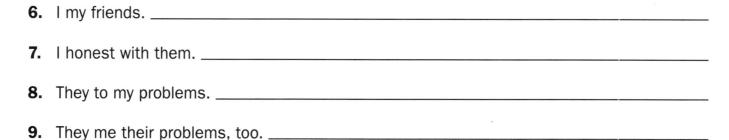

Once my mother believed everything I told her. Then one day, I a lie. I about where I was going. I said I was going to the library. Instead, I to the bookstore. I my friends there. We talked and looked at magazines. My mother was hurt by my dishonesty. I honest with her now.

Proofreader's Marks

Add text:
am
I ⌃ sorry.

See all Proofreader's Marks on page ix.

B. Write each fragment as a complete sentence. Add a verb.

6. I my friends. _____

7. I honest with them. _____

8. They to my problems. _____

9. They me their problems, too. _____

C. Answer the questions. Write complete sentences. Be sure each sentence has a verb.

10. Whom do you trust? _____

_____

11. Who trusts and believes in you? _____

_____

12. What action would cause you to distrust someone? _____

_____

D. (13–14) Why is it hard to rebuild trust after it is lost? Write at least two complete sentences that tell why. Remember to use a verb in each sentence.

_____

_____

_____

_____

Edit It

E. (15–20) Edit the note. Fix six mistakes. Add a verb to make each sentence complete.

Mom,

    I am sorry that I lied to you. Your trust important to me. I promise to be truthful. I also to confide in you. You and Dad important to me. I know that you about me. I also about you. I I can rebuild the trust you once had in me.

Love,

Juanita

Proofreader's Marks
Add text:
care
I know you ⌃ about me.

14 What's One More Way to Fix a Fragment?

Combine Neighboring Sentences.

Writers may create a fragment by starting a new sentence when they shouldn't. These fragments are easy to fix.
Just combine the fragment with the sentence before it.

┌─── sentence ───┐ ┌────── fragment ──────┐
1. Joe saves his money.   Because he wants to buy tickets.
Joe saves his money because he wants to buy tickets.

┌─── sentence ───┐ ┌──── fragment ────┐
2. Joe buys the tickets.   And offers one to me.
Joe buys the tickets and offers one to me.

Try It

A. **Find each fragment. Combine it with the sentence. Write the new sentence.**

1. Joe tells me. That the tickets are in the front row. _____
   _____

2. We go to the concert. And look for our seats. _____
   _____

3. I am disappointed. When we find our seats. _____
   _____

4. Joe exaggerated. Because he wanted me to think they were good seats. _____
   _____

B. **(5–9) Draw a line to combine each sentence with a fragment.**

Joe wants attention.	Because he wants to make things look better.
Joe exaggerates.	So he tries to impress people.
I always believe Joe.	Because he acts so sincere.
People have learned.	But it is a serious problem.
Joe laughs it off.	That they can't trust Joe.

C. Answer the questions about exaggerating. Be sure to write complete sentences.

10. Do you think it is ever appropriate to exaggerate? Why or why not? I think _____

_____.

11. How do you feel about people who exaggerate? I feel _____

_____.

12. Why might someone exaggerate? Someone might _____

_____.

D. (13–15) Imagine you have a friend who exaggerates. Would you stop your friend from trying to make things seem bigger and better than they are? Write at least three sentences to tell what you would say or do.

_____

_____

_____

_____

Edit It

E. (16–20) Edit the note. Fix five fragments.

Hi Parker,

I just got a note from Joe. He says he has tickets to a hockey game. He says. That he knows the players. He says. That he will introduce me to them after the game. I can't believe him. Because he always exaggerates. He will probably cancel the invitation. When it gets close to game time. What do you think I should do?

Give me a call. When you have time.

Jason

Proofreader's Marks

Do not capitalize:

I'll see you at the hockey ~~G~~ame.

Delete:

I am going ~~to~~ to the game.

See all Proofreader's Marks on page ix.

15 Fix Sentence Fragments

Remember: You can fix a fragment by adding a subject or a predicate that includes a verb. Or, you can combine the fragment with another sentence.

Fragment:	Tell me what to do.
Sentence:	Many people tell me what to do.
Fragment:	I to be independent.
Sentence:	I want to be independent.
Fragment:	I make good decisions. Because I know myself well.
Sentence:	I make good decisions because I know myself well.

Try It

A. Fix the fragments. Write complete sentences.

1. Dad tells me what to do. Whenever he wants. _____

_____

2. I appreciate his advice. Because he is really smart. _____

_____

3. Still like to make my own decisions. _____

4. Independence very important to me. _____

5. I am learning about life. And other teenagers are, too. _____

_____

6. My mother was independent. When she was young. _____

_____

7. She worked hard. Because she lived on a ranch. _____

_____

B. Draw a line under the fragment. Then combine it with the sentence. Write the new sentence.

8. She learned to ride. And rope cattle.

_____

9. She learned from her father. When to feed the cattle.

_____

10. I hope to be just like my mother. When I am older.

_____

Write It

C. Answer the questions. Be sure to write complete sentences.

11. What do you think it means to be independent? I think _____.

12. Who are some independent people you admire? _____

_____

D. (13–15) Now write at least three sentences to tell how you think teenagers can achieve independence while still living at home.

_____

_____

_____

Edit It

E. (16–20) Edit the paragraph. Fix five fragments.

I like science. I study biology. Because I want to work near the ocean. I live. With my parents and grandparents. Are very supportive of me. I think every teenager goals. Without goals, I can't be independent. My goals very important to me.

Proofreader's Marks
Do not capitalize:
I live near the Øcean.
Add text:
listen
I to my parents.
∧
Delete:
I am going home.
See all Proofreader's Marks on page ix.

✓ Capitalize the First Word in a Sentence and the Pronoun *I*

Capital letters provide important visual clues to readers. Use a capital letter to show where a sentence begins.

- Capitalize the first word in a sentence.

   We eat vegetables every night. **Some** of my favorite foods are vegetables.

- Capitalize the personal pronoun **I**, even when it is not the first word in a sentence. Do not capitalize other personal pronouns, unless they are the first word in a sentence.

   Potatoes and carrots are the ones **I** like best. My aunt makes the best mashed potatoes. **I** think **she** is a great cook.

Try It

A. Use proofreader's marks to correct the capitalization error in each sentence.

1. Hamburgers are still my favorite food, but i also like vegetables.

2. My brother does not like vegetables. he does not even like lettuce.

3. Our neighbor brought over grilled eggplant. The flavor was unusual, but It really was not too bad.

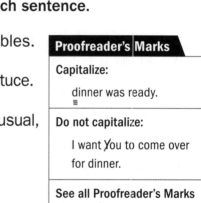

Proofreader's Marks

Capitalize:

dinner was ready.
≡

Do not capitalize:

I want Ɏou to come over for dinner.

See all Proofreader's Marks on page ix.

B. (4–10) Edit the story. Find and fix seven capitalization errors.

   I used to think vegetables were boring, but one day i discovered something different. Our family was invited to Our neighbors' cookout. Mr. and Mrs. Manning made hamburgers, hot dogs, and roasted vegetables. I was ready for a juicy hamburger but not the roasted vegetables. i was secretly hoping to skip the tasteless vegetables.

   Mrs. Manning gave Me a hamburger and then added some roasted potatoes and red peppers to my plate. Now i had to try them. I slowly took a bite. the first bite proved to be very tasty. Within minutes, i ate all my vegetables and forgot about my juicy hamburger!

✓ Add End Punctuation Correctly

- Use a period at the end of a sentence or a polite command. You should also use a period at the end of a statement that includes a question.

    Our neighbors invited us for **dinner.** Let's **go.**

    "Have you ever tried fried green tomatoes**?**" Mrs. Triche **asked.**

- Use a question mark at the end of a direct question.

    Who ever heard of fried green **tomatoes?**

- Use an exclamation point to show strong feelings or surprise.

    Wow! These tomatoes are really **good!**

Try It

A. (11–15) Edit the story. Find and fix five punctuation errors.

I couldn't wait until lunchtime Our cooking class had prepared a special lunch. We invited our friends to taste our special meal. Would they like what we made

My friend Marc was the first in line. "Do you like spinach?" I asked him He looked disappointed. "I'm not a big fan of spinach, but I'll try it," he replied. Imagine his surprise when we started to serve spinach pizzas. "Wow This is delicious!" he exclaimed

Proofreader's Marks

Add a period:

I like hamburgers⌄

Add a question mark:

Do you like vegetables?⌄

Add an exclamation point:

These carrots are great!⌄

B. Write sentences about food you like and food you don't like. Use the correct end punctuation for the type of sentence listed.

16. (sentence) _____

17. (question) _____

18. (sentence with strong feelings or surprise) _____

19. (question) _____

20. (statement with a question) _____

✓ Check Your Spelling

Homonyms are words that sound alike but have different meanings and spellings. Spell these homonyms correctly when you proofread.

Homonyms and Their Meanings	Examples
it's (contraction) = it is; it has	**It's** important to eat plenty of vegetables.
its (adjective) = belonging to it	I noticed **its** flavor.
there (adverb) = that place or position	They planted tomatoes **there**.
their (adjective) = belonging to them	**Their** garden is full of vegetables.
they're (contraction) = they are	**They're** excellent gardeners.

Try It

A. Complete each sentence about gardens. Use the correct homonym.

21. They were working in _____ garden today.
    there / their / they're

22. _____ great that they grow their own vegetables.
    It's / Its

23. _____ always giving us tomatoes and other vegetables to try.
    There / Their / They're

24. One day they gave me a strange-looking potato. I noticed _____
    it's / its
    dark purple color.

B. (25–30) Tell a brief story about trying a new food. Write six sentences. Use at least one homonym in each sentence.

_____

_____

_____

_____

_____

_____

✓ Check Sentences for Completeness

A sentence is complete when it expresses a complete thought and has two parts:
the **subject** and the **predicate**. A **subject** tells who. A **predicate** tells what the
subject does. Every predicate needs a **verb**.

Problem	Solution
1. Sentence is missing a subject.	**Add the missing subject.**
Still eat hamburgers.	**I** still eat hamburgers.
2. Sentence is missing a verb.	**Add the missing verb.**
I also salads.	I also **make** salads.
3. Sentence fragments do not express a complete thought.	**Join the fragments to express a complete thought.**
Just one dinner. Changed my opinion of vegetables.	Just one dinner changed my opinion of vegetables.

Try It

A. Tell the problem in each sentence. Then rewrite it to make it a complete sentence.

31. Dinner soon ready. _____

_____

32. Saw the plate of vegetables and didn't know what to do. _____

_____

33. I wanted. To throw it away. _____

_____

34. Instead, I a small bite, then another, and another. _____

_____

35. To my surprise, I liked. The roasted tomatoes and the sweet red peppers. _____

_____

_____

16 Is the Subject of a Sentence Always a Noun?

No, It Can Be a Pronoun.

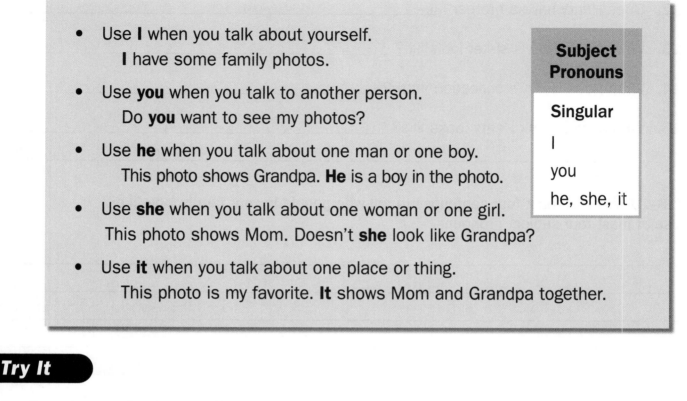

- Use **I** when you talk about yourself.
  I have some family photos.

- Use **you** when you talk to another person.
  Do **you** want to see my photos?

- Use **he** when you talk about one man or one boy.
  This photo shows Grandpa. **He** is a boy in the photo.

- Use **she** when you talk about one woman or one girl.
  This photo shows Mom. Doesn't **she** look like Grandpa?

- Use **it** when you talk about one place or thing.
  This photo is my favorite. **It** shows Mom and Grandpa together.

Subject Pronouns
Singular
I
you
he, she, it

Try It

A. Complete each sentence. Use a subject pronoun from the chart above.

1. My name is Henry. _____ have a brother and a sister.

2. Zac is my brother. _____ looks like my dad.

3. Sara is my sister. _____ looks like my mom.

4. Do _____ think I look like my mom or my dad?

B. (5–11) Complete the paragraph. Use subject pronouns from the chart.

Henry is working on a school project. _____ is a collection of

family photos. _____ will use his favorite photos. Henry asks his mom,

"Will _____ help with the collection?" "Yes, _____ will,"

_____ answers.

When the collection is finished, Henry looks at it. _____ can see a

resemblance among all the members of his family. "_____ look a little

like everyone," he says.

C. Answer these questions about Henry. Use the correct subject pronouns.

12. Does Henry have a brother? _____

13. Who does Henry's sister look like? _____

14. What does Henry's collection show? _____

15. Who do you think Henry looks like? _____

_____

D. (16–19) Write at least four sentences to tell who people in your family look like. Use at least four subject pronouns.

_____

_____

_____

_____

_____

Edit It

E. (20–25) Edit the letter. Fix six mistakes.

Dear Grandma,
   I am studying genetics in school. He is very interesting.
   Did he know that a gene is an instruction to your body?
She contains DNA. Genes determine people's traits. It got
some genes from Mom. He got some from you. That's
why it look like you!
Love,
Henry

Proofreader's Marks
Change text: 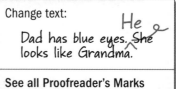
Dad has blue eyes. She looks like Grandma.
See all Proofreader's Marks on page ix.

17 Can a Pronoun Show "More Than One"?
Yes, It Can.

- Use **we** to talk about yourself and another person.

    My sister and I are going to England this summer.
    We will visit our grandparents on Mom's side.

- Use **you** to talk to one or more persons.

    "Elaine, do **you** like to travel with your sister?"
    my friend asked.
    "**You** should buy matching luggage," he said.

- Use **they** to talk about more than one person or thing.

    My cousins will be in England, too. **They** live there.

Subject Pronouns	
Singular	**Plural**
I	we
you	you
he, she, it	they

Try It

A. **Complete the sentences. Use the correct plural subject pronouns.**

1. Anna and I just got off the plane. _____ are in England now.

2. Our grandparents see us. _____ wave.

3. "_____ have really grown, Elaine," says Grandma to me.

4. "_____ are both so tall," says Grandpa to Anna and me.

5. We take after Dad's parents. _____ are tall, too.

B. **(6–10) Complete the paragraph about the girls. Use the correct plural subject pronouns.**

Anna and I just met our cousins for the first time. _____ are

surprised because _____ look a lot like us. Genes are pretty amazing,

I guess. _____ determine how we look. "Anna, did _____ ever

imagine we could look so much like our cousins?" I ask.

"I guess it's because _____ all have the same grandparents!" she says.

C. Answer these questions that Elaine might ask you. Use correct plural
subject pronouns.

11. Where do Mom's parents live? _____

12. Where do Anna and I get our height? _____

13. What do genes do? _____

D. (14–17) Write at least four sentences to tell about your extended family. How
are you all alike and different? Use at least four plural subject pronouns.

_____

_____

_____

_____

_____

Edit It

E. (18–25) Edit the paragraph. Fix eight mistakes.

My cousins and I are alike in some ways. You are all
athletic. My cousins are runners. I think you inherited
that ability from Grandpa. My sister and I aren't runners.
They are javelin throwers. I think they inherited that
ability from Grandma. "Do he think our athletic abilities
are inherited?" I asked my cousins. "You think so,"
they answered, "and I are lucky to have such talented
grandparents. You passed strong abilities to us."

Proofreader's Marks

Change text:

Grandpa and Grandma
are tall. ^They She passed that
trait on to us.

See all Proofreader's Marks
on page ix.

18 Are There Different Subject Pronouns for Men and Women?

Yes, There Are.

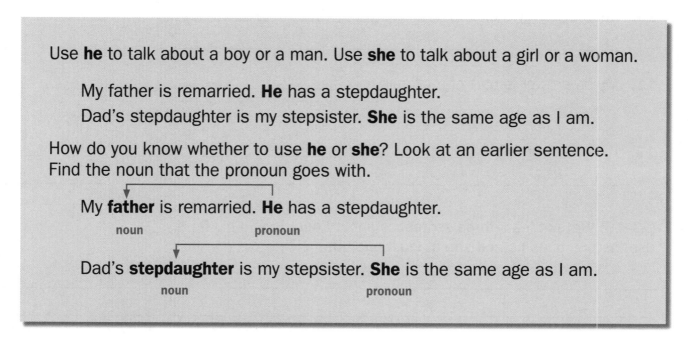

Use **he** to talk about a boy or a man. Use **she** to talk about a girl or a woman.

> My father is remarried. **He** has a stepdaughter.
> Dad's stepdaughter is my stepsister. **She** is the same age as I am.

How do you know whether to use **he** or **she**? Look at an earlier sentence. Find the noun that the pronoun goes with.

My **father** is remarried. **He** has a stepdaughter.
noun   pronoun

Dad's **stepdaughter** is my stepsister. **She** is the same age as I am.
noun   pronoun

Try It

A. Complete each second sentence with the correct subject pronoun.
Then underline the noun that the pronoun goes with.

1. My stepmom is really nice. _____ and I get along well.

2. Dad thinks I look like her. _____ says we have the same eyes.

3. Stephanie is my stepsister. _____ is becoming one of my best friends.

4. My brother says that Stephanie and I are two of a kind. _____ says we are even starting to look alike!

B. (5–9) Complete the paragraph about Eduardo. Use the correct subject pronouns.

Eduardo lives in a blended family, too. _____ was adopted a few years ago. That's why _____ doesn't share physical traits with his mom. Eduardo's mom got remarried last year. So now _____ is a stepmother. Her stepdaughter has brown eyes and brown hair. _____ shares those traits with Eduardo. _____ likes to sing, just like Eduardo.

C. Read the sentence. Then write a second sentence that uses the pronoun
he or **she**.

10. Eduardo is my friend. _____

_____

11. My stepsister is part of my family. _____

_____

12. Kyle is my brother. _____

_____

D. (13–15) Write at least three sentences about Eduardo and his family.
Use the pronouns **he** and **she** at least one time each.

_____

_____

_____

_____

Edit It

E. (16–20) Edit the journal entry. Fix five subject pronouns.

June 19

Today, I met my baby cousin Ben for the
first time. She is my aunt Sophia's first
baby. She adopted Ben. It is a very cute
baby. When Ben smiles, they reminds me of
Aunt Sophia. Aunt Sophia smiles all the time
because he is so happy with her new baby. I
am looking forward to babysitting for Ben.
When she gets older, I want to teach him
everything I know!

Proofreader's Marks

Change text:

He
~~It~~ is part of my
extended family.

See all Proofreader's Marks
on page ix.

⑲ How Do You Avoid Confusion with Pronouns?

Match the Pronoun to the Noun.

To make your sentences clear, match the pronouns to the nouns.

Unclear: Diego is busy. **It** is making a family tree.

Clear: Diego is busy. **He** is making a family tree.

First, find the noun the pronoun goes with. Then ask yourself:

Is the noun plural or singular? If plural, use **they**. If singular, ask:

Is the noun a man, a woman, or a thing? Use **he** for a man, **she** for a woman, and **it** for a place or thing.

The pronouns in these sentences are correct. Do you know why?

1. Diego's **mom** helps. **She** tells about her family.
     noun   pronoun

2. Diego's **dad** helps, too. **He** tells about his family.
     noun   pronoun

3. Both **parents** have many relatives. **They** come from big families.
     noun   pronoun

Try It

A. **Write the correct pronoun to complete the second sentence.**

1. Diego's great-grandparents grew up in Mexico. _____ moved to California.
                                                                    He / They

2. Diego's grandmother was born there. _____ grew up in Los Angeles.
                                                            It / She

3. Diego's father went to college in Boston. _____ met Diego's mother there.
                                                                He / She

4. Diego and his siblings live in the U.S. _____ have never been to Mexico.
                                                              It / They

5. This summer, Diego's grandmother is taking Diego to Mexico. _____
                                                                              She / They
   will introduce him to his Mexican relatives.

B. (6–13) Write the correct subject pronouns to complete the paragraph about Diego.

Before Diego goes to Mexico, _____ wants to study his family tree. _____ shows his relatives in Mexico. _____ all live in different parts of the country. Maria is his grandmother's cousin. _____ lives in Mexico City. Her son, Miguel, lives in Acapulco. _____ works in a hotel on the beach there.

Diego feels very lucky. _____ will travel all over Mexico and meet his extended family. Will his relatives look like him? Will _____ have the same interests? The trip will be fun. _____ will be a learning experience, too.

Write It

C. Complete the first sentence about your family. Write a second sentence that uses the pronoun **he**, **she**, **it**, or **they**.

14. My family _____.

_____

_____

15. My grandfather _____.

_____

_____

16. _____ is my cousin. _____

_____

_____

D. (17–20) Write at least four sentences about other relatives in your extended family. Use each of the pronouns **he**, **she**, and **they** at least once.

_____

_____

_____

_____

_____

20 Use Subject Pronouns

Remember: The subject of a sentence can be a pronoun.
A **subject pronoun** can be singular or plural.

- Use **I** when you talk about yourself.
- Use **you** to talk to one or more persons.
- Use **we** to talk about another person and yourself.
- Use **he**, **she**, **it**, and **they** to talk about other people or things.

   How do you know which pronoun to use? Look at the noun it goes with.
   1. If the noun is a man or boy, use **he**.
      If it is a woman or girl, use **she**.

   2. If the noun is a place or thing, use **it**.
      If the noun is plural, use **they**.

Try It

A. Write the correct subject pronoun to complete the second sentence.

1. My name is Joshua. _____ live in New Hampshire.

I / You

2. My family and I are going to New York. _____ will attend a big family

She / We
   reunion at my grandma's house.

3. My cousin Matthew is my age. _____ looks a lot like me.

I / He

4. Matthew and I both have blond hair. _____ both have blue eyes, too.

You / We

B. (5–8) Write the correct subject pronouns to complete the paragraph.

   My grandma likes to garden. _____ grows beautiful flowers. "Joshua,"
she asks me, "would _____ like to learn about my flowers?" "Yes,
_____ would," I say. Her flowers are a little like my family. _____
all are flowers, but like my family, some of them look the same, and others look
very different.

C. Answer these questions about the family reunion. Use subject pronouns in your answers.

9. Where is the reunion? _____

10. Who does Joshua look like? Why? _____

_____

11. What does Joshua's grandma like to do? _____

12. How do you think Joshua's grandparents feel when their family comes to the reunion?

_____

D. (13–17) Write at least five sentences to tell about a reunion for your family. Who will come? Whom do you share traits with? Use at least five subject pronouns.

_____

_____

_____

_____

_____

E. (18–25) Edit the letter. Fix eight pronouns.

Dear Grandma and Grandpa,

Thanks so much for inviting us to the reunion. We were happy to come. He had a really good time. It enjoyed seeing Matthew. She has changed so much since last year. Do it think that Matthew and I look alike? I think you look more like brothers than cousins! Thank me for showing me how to plant flowers. I planted flowers at home. It look beautiful. Mom likes them, too. They says now you have passed on your good looks to me and your love of gardening, too.

Love,

Joshua

Proofreader's Marks

Change text:

Grandpa and Grandma had a reunion. ~~She~~ They invited the whole family.

See all Proofreader's Marks on page ix.

21 What Adds Action to a Sentence?

An Action Verb

- An **action verb** tells what the subject does.
  Some action verbs tell about an action that you cannot see.
    Our family **enjoys** food.
    Good meals **bring** us together.

- Make sure the action verb agrees with its subject. Add **-s** if the
  subject tells about one place, one thing, or one other person.
    Grandma **bakes** the best cookies.
    Her grandchildren **help** her.
    The cookies **taste** delicious.
    Dad **eats** them for a snack.

Try It

A. Write an action verb to complete each sentence about Julia.

   1. Julia's aunts _____ food all the time.

   2. Julia _____ to cook, too.

   3. Today, Julia and her aunts _____ lasagna.

   4. The lasagna _____ in the oven.

   5. The cooks _____ lasagna to the whole family.

B. Write the correct form of the verb in parentheses to complete each sentence
about cooking.

   6. Many parents _____ their children to know how to cook. **(want)**

   7. The children _____ to cook healthy meals. **(learn)**

   8. In Julia's family, each child _____ one healthy dinner a week. **(cook)**

   9. Each parent _____ one healthy dinner, too. **(make)**

   10. Then, all the family members _____ the healthy meal together. **(eat)**

C. Imagine that Julia's family is making dinner together. Use the subject and the correct form of the verb in parentheses to tell about the meal.

11. Julia's family (**prepare**) _____

12. Her brothers (**slice**) _____

13. Julia's parents (**grill**) _____

14. Julia (**set**) _____

D. (15–18) What do you learn from your relatives? Write at least four sentences to tell what they show you to do. Use at least four action verbs. Make sure each verb agrees with the subject.

_____

_____

_____

_____

_____

Edit It

E. (19 –25) Edit the cooking directions. Use proofreader's marks to correct the subject-verb agreement if it is incorrect.

How Julia's Family Makes a Salad
1. Julia rinse all the vegetables.
2. Brad and Roy peels the carrots.
3. Mom cuts all the vegetables.
4. Dad make a salad dressing.
5. The brothers puts everything in a bowl.
6. Mom stir everything together.
7. The family eats.

Proofreader's Marks

Change text:

Dad ~~love~~ to cook.
loves

See all Proofreader's Marks on page ix.

㉒ How Do You Know When the Action Happens?
Look at the Verb.

An **action verb** tells what the subject does. The tense of a verb tells when the action happens.

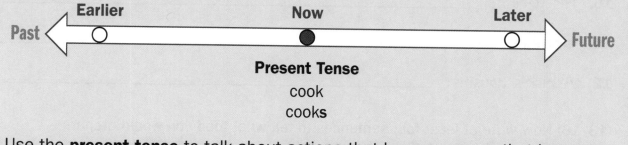

Use the **present tense** to talk about actions that happen now or that happen on a regular basis.

Ashish **cooks** for his grandmother. His grandmother **enjoys** the meals. His parents **eat** with Ashish and his grandmother.

Try It

A. Underline the present tense action verb in each sentence. Then write a different present tense verb for the sentence.

1. Ashish's grandmother lives alone. _____

2. Sometimes she needs help with her meals. _____

3. Her children make dinners for her. _____

4. Her grandchildren bring her lunch. _____

B. Complete each sentence with a present tense verb from the box.

drive	make	sit	taste

5. Today, Ashish _____ chicken soup for Grandma.

6. His parents _____ Ashish to Grandma's apartment to give her the soup.

7. The family members _____ around the table.

8. The soup _____ delicious.

C. Complete the sentences to tell about a dessert that Ashish makes for his grandmother. Use present tense verbs that match the subjects.

9. After dinner, Ashish _____.

10. His parents _____.

11. Grandma _____.

12. Ashish's cousins _____.

D. (13–16) Now write at least four sentences to tell what food you would prepare to help out one of your relatives. Use at least four present tense verbs.

_____

_____

_____

_____

_____

Edit It

E. (17–25) Verbs are missing from this paragraph that tells how Ashish helps out today. Edit the paragraph to add nine present tense verbs.

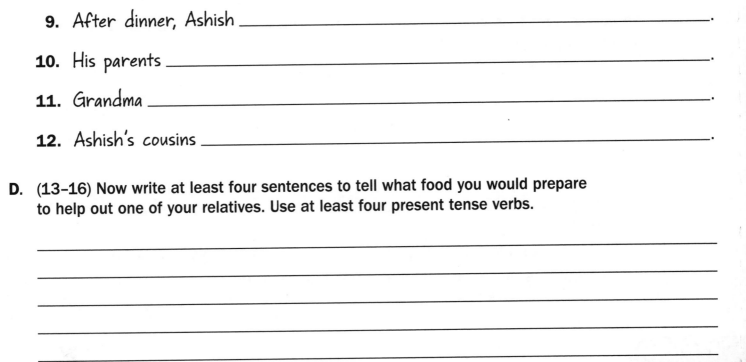

Ashish walks to Aunt Liat's house. Aunt Liat and Ashish to the grocery store. Aunt Liat groceries. They the groceries to Grandma's house. Grandma the groceries away. Then Grandma, Ashish, and Aunt Liat a snack. Ashish the snack. Grandma all the delicious snacks. Finally, Aunt Liat and Ashish good-bye and home.

Proofreader's Marks

Add text:
Grandma ∧ help.
  needs

See all Proofreader's Marks on page ix.

© National Geographic Learning, a part of Cengage Learning, Inc.

23 Which Action Verbs End in -*s*?

The Ones That Go with *He*, *She*, or *It*

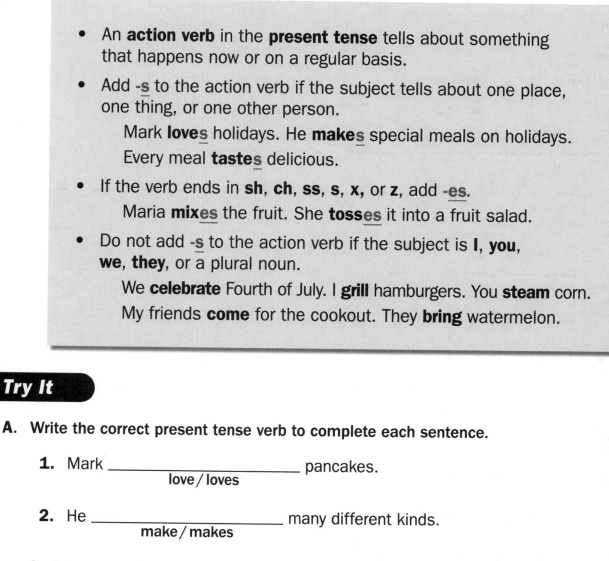

- An **action verb** in the **present tense** tells about something that happens now or on a regular basis.

- Add -<u>s</u> to the action verb if the subject tells about one place, one thing, or one other person.

    Mark **love<u>s</u>** holidays. He **make<u>s</u>** special meals on holidays.
    Every meal **tastes** delicious.

- If the verb ends in **sh**, **ch**, **ss**, **s**, **x**, or **z**, add -<u>es</u>.

    Maria **mix<u>es</u>** the fruit. She **toss<u>es</u>** it into a fruit salad.

- Do not add -<u>s</u> to the action verb if the subject is **I**, **you**, **we**, **they**, or a plural noun.

    We **celebrate** Fourth of July. I **grill** hamburgers. You **steam** corn.
    My friends **come** for the cookout. They **bring** watermelon.

Try It

A. Write the correct present tense verb to complete each sentence.

1. Mark _____ pancakes.
       love / loves

2. He _____ many different kinds.
      make / makes

3–4. I _____ I _____ them all.
         think / thinks   like / likes

5. Mom _____ the banana pancakes.
       enjoy / enjoys

6. Today, Mom _____ her birthday.
       celebrate / celebrates

7. We _____ a surprise breakfast for her.
      plan / plans

8. Mark _____ a batch of banana pancakes.
       mix / mixes

9. My sisters _____ them out. Yum!
       dish / dishes

B. Choose words from each column to build six sentences about favorite foods for special occasions. You can use words more than once.

Sue	grills	cookies for Valentine's Day.
Ralph	broil	hamburgers for Memorial Day.
We	want	corn on the cob for graduation.
My cousins	serves	vegetables on Labor Day.
You	prepares	steak on our parents' anniversary.
She	bake	ice-cream cake on our birthdays.

10. _____

11. _____

12. _____

13. _____

14. _____

15. _____

Write It

C. Answer the questions about your favorite occasion. Use action verbs.

16. What is your favorite occasion? I _____.

17. What special meal does your family prepare for you on that occasion? My family _____
_____.

18. How do they cook your favorite food? They _____
_____.

D. (19–20) Write at least two sentences to tell about a favorite treat that you and your family share. Use action verbs correctly.

_____

_____

_____

24 What Kinds of Verbs Are *Can, Could, May,* and *Might*?

They Are Helping Verbs.

- An action verb can have two parts: a **helping verb** and a **main verb**. The main verb shows the action.

    I buy groceries for Mom. I **can buy** groceries for Mom.

- Some helping verbs change the meaning of the action verb.

    1. Use **can** or **could** to tell about an ability.

    Dad **can drive** me to the market. He **could drive** you, too.

    2. Use **may, might**, or **could** to tell about a possibility.

    My sister **may shop** for food with me. My brother **might come**, too. We **could go** to the store together.

- **Can, could, may,** and **might** stay the same with all subjects. Do not add **-s**.

    Mom **appreciates** our help. She **can rest** now. She **might take** a nap.

Try It

A. Write **can, could, may,** or **might** to complete each sentence. More than one answer is possible.

1. Aunt Rosita works full time, so she _____ use a lot of help.

2. Oscar _____ help Aunt Rosita a little every day.

3. On one day, he _____ make lunch for her children.

4. On another day, he _____ prepare dinner.

5. His cousins _____ like the dinner.

6. If they don't like it, they _____ ask to order pizza.

B. Rewrite each sentence. Add **can**, **could**, **may**, or **might**. More than one answer is possible.

7. Oscar cleans the kitchen for Aunt Rosita. _____

_____

8. His cousins help him. _____

_____

9. Then Oscar reads them a story. _____

_____

10. They fall asleep. _____

_____.

Write It

C. Complete the sentences to tell what other things Oscar and his family could do to help Aunt Rosita. Use **can**, **could**, **may**, or **might** in each sentence.

11. Oscar _____.

12. Oscar's parents _____.

13. Oscar's grandmother _____.

14. Oscar's siblings _____.

15. How might Aunt Rosita show her appreciation? She _____

_____.

D. (16–20) How could you help out your family members? How might they show their appreciation for your help? Write at least five sentences. Use **can**, **could**, **may**, or **might**.

_____

_____

_____

_____

_____

25 Use Action Verbs in the Present Tense

Remember: A verb must agree with its subject.

- Some subjects use **-s** on the **action verb**.

I **graduate** today.	He **graduates** today.
You **attend** the graduation.	She **attends** graduation.
The students **smile**.	The student **smiles**.
They **receive** diplomas.	Alex **receives** a diploma.

- **These verbs don't change.**

  She **may celebrate** after graduation.

  He **could take** her out to lunch.

  It **might be** a surprise.

Try It

A. Write the correct present tense verb or helping verb to complete each sentence.

1. After today, my brother Alex _____ sleep late.
   can / cans

2. That's because he _____ high school today.
   finish / finishes

3. The graduation _____ place at 10 in the morning.
   take / takes

4. The graduates _____ caps and gowns.
   wear / wears

5. All the families _____ for them.
   applaud / applauds

B. (6–10) Write present tense verbs or helping verbs to complete the paragraph.

My parents _____ a celebration for Alex. They _____ our whole extended family. Each person _____ one of Alex's favorite foods. Uncle Joe _____ chicken. Alex _____ Uncle Joe's grilled chicken better than any other food in the world!

C. What might Alex's family members bring to the celebration meal? Write sentences to explain. Use a different present tense verb in each sentence.

11. Alex's grandparents _____.

12. Aunt Gert _____.

13. Alex's younger brother _____.

14. Cousin Arthur _____.

D. (15–19) What special occasion does your family celebrate? Write at least five sentences about how your family celebrates the occasion. Use present tense verbs.

_____

_____

_____

_____

_____

E. (20–25) Edit Alex's journal entry. Fix six present tense or helping verbs.

June 6
Today, I graduate from high school. I
coulds jump for joy, but Mom feel a little
sad and nostalgic. My teachers presents
awards at the graduation ceremony. The
principal give out diplomas. My family loves
celebrations, and they loves to eat, too.
That's why we're having a huge meal to
celebrates my graduation!

Proofreader's Marks

Change text:
writes
Alex write about
graduation.

See all Proofreader's Marks on page ix.

26 What Forms of *Be* Are Used in the Present?

Am, Is, and *Are*

- Use the form of the verb **be** that matches the subject.

  I **am** from the United States.

  My mom **is** from Vietnam.

  Her sister came with her to the U.S. They **are** Vietnamese and American.

  We **are** part of both cultures.

Present Tense Forms of *Be*
I **am**
he, she, or it **is**
we, you, or they **are**

- Use **not** after the verbs **am**, **is**, and **are** to make a sentence negative. The short form of **is not** is **isn't**. The short form of **are not** is **aren't**.

  1. Dad **is not** from Vietnam.

  Dad **isn't** from Vietnam.

  2. My parents **are not** from the U.S.

  My parents **aren't** from the U.S.

Try It

A. Write the correct verb form to complete each sentence.

1. I _____ from a multicultural neighborhood.
         am / are

2. We _____ all alike in many ways.
         is / are

3. The parents _____ all from the United States, though.
              isn't / aren't

4. Each background culture _____ different.
                   is / are

B. (5–10) Complete the paragraph. Use the correct form of **be**.

Julio's parents _____ from Colombia. They _____ speakers of both Spanish and English. Julio _____, too. I _____ able to speak Vietnamese, but my father can't. He _____ a speaker of Vietnamese. French _____ his native language.

C. Complete sentences that tell about neighbors in a multicultural neighborhood. Use a form of **be** in each sentence.

11. My next-door neighbors come from Italy. They _____.

12. Their son learns to _____ from them. He _____.

13. I learn from my parents, too. I _____.

14. All children learn a lot from parents. Customs _____.

D. (15–18) Write at least four sentences to tell how your family's culture influences you. Use the correct form of **be** at least four times.

_____

_____

_____

_____

_____

Edit It

E. (19–25) Edit the interview. Use proofreader's marks to fix seven mistakes with verbs.

Q: Your parents aren't from Canada, are they?

A: No, they is from Greece. They live in New York now.

Q: How does their culture affect you?

A: Mom are a great cook. She makes Greek food. I are excited about learning how to cook Greek food, too. Dad aren't such a good cook, but he am a great Greek folk dancer. He are teaching me. Now I is a good dancer, too!

Proofreader's Marks

Change text:

Greek, am Dad's native language.
(is ∘)

See all Proofreader's Marks on page ix.

27 How Do You Show That an Action Is in Process?

Use Am, Is, or Are plus the -ing Form of the Verb.

- The **present progressive** form of the verb ends in **-ing**.
- Use **am**, **is**, or **are** plus a **main verb** with **-ing** to show that an action is in the process of happening. The **helping verb** must agree with the subject.

  Mom **is** go**ing** to work.

  I **am** go**ing** with her.

  She **is** show**ing** me what she does at work.

  Her coworkers **are** tell**ing** me about their jobs, too.

Try It

A. (1–5) Write the correct present progressive verb to complete each sentence about career day.

We _____ a career day at school. Many parents
　　　　am having / are having

_____ information about their jobs. I _____
is sharing / are sharing　　　　　　　　　　　　　　am listening / are listening

carefully. My mom _____ her job as an engineer. She
　　　　　　is describing / are describing

_____ about designing computer software.
is telling / are telling

B. Write the present progressive form of the verb in parentheses.

6. Sonya's mom _____ about her job as a surgeon. **(talk)**

7. I _____ close attention. **(pay)**

8. I _____ about going to medical school. **(think)**

9. My parents _____ me follow my dream. **(help)**

10. They _____ that I volunteer at the hospital. **(hope)**

C. Complete the sentences to tell about careers at your school. Use the present progressive to tell what each person is doing.

11. The custodians _____.

12. The secretary _____.

13. My teachers _____.

14. Our principal _____.

D. (15–18) Write at least four sentences to tell where would you like to work someday. Use present progressive verbs.

_____

_____

_____

_____

_____

Edit It

E. (19–25) Edit the school newspaper report about career day. Use proofreader's marks to fix seven present progressive verbs.

High School Career Day

Today, the students are learning about careers. Many parents is discuss their jobs. One dad is talk about his career as a city bus driver. He are telling about his route. Two moms are explain how they decided to become police officers. They needed a lot of training.

"I is enjoying this career day," said student Jake Bloom. "It are help me think about what I want to do when I finish school. I is plan to be a police officer, too."

Proofreader's Marks

Change text:

Mom ~~am~~ is studying engineering.

See all Proofreader's Marks on page ix.

28 What Forms of *Have* Are Used in the Present?

Have and Has

Use the form of the verb **have** that matches the subject.

- I **have** healthy parents.
- She **has** healthy parents, too.
- They **have** great ideas about how to stay healthy.
- We **have** healthy habits.
- Do you **have** time to go for a walk now?

Present Tense Forms of *Have*
I **have**
he, she, or it **has**
we, you, or they **have**

Try It

A. Write the correct form of **have** to complete each sentence.

1. My mom _____ a bicycle.
   have / has

2. I _____ one, too.
   have / has

3. We _____ fun when we ride our bikes together.
   have / has

4. Today, she _____ the day off from work.
   have / has

5. Our family _____ a plan.
   have / has

B. (6–10) Complete the paragraph about the plan. Use the correct form of **have**.

Our plan _____ something to do with bicycles. It _____

something to do with exercise, too. Do you _____ an idea what our

plan is? That's right! My family and I _____ a bicycle trip to go on! The

tires _____ air in them, and we are ready to go.

Write It

C. Complete the sentences to tell how family members might stay fit and healthy. Use the correct form of **have** to tell about their interests.

11. The parents _____.

12. One son _____.

13. The daughter _____.

14. We all _____.

D. (15–18) Write at least four sentences to tell what you or your family does to stay fit and healthy. Use a form of **have** at least four times.

_____

_____

_____

_____

_____

Edit It

E. (19–25) **Have** and **has** are missing from this list of things Felix needs to do. Edit the list to make seven corrections by adding **have** or **has**.

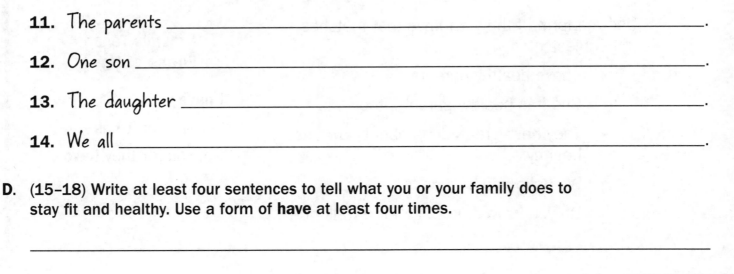

To Do List

1. Rena has a track meet. I a car so I will drive her to the meet.

2. My brother's bike a flat tire. It a leak. I need to fix it.

3. My basketball team a game tomorrow. We a mandatory practice at 4 o'clock.

4. I math homework. I need to finish 25 exercises. I to work fast.

Proofreader's Marks

Add text:

My family a busy schedule. _{has}

See all Proofreader's Marks on page ix.

29 What Forms of *Do* Are Used in the Present?

Do and *Does*

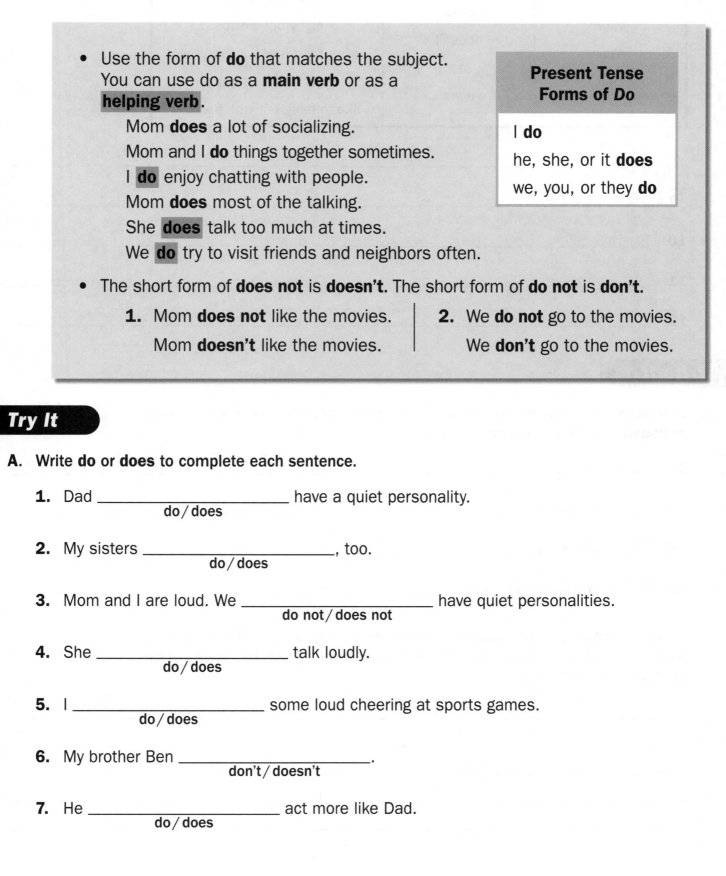

- Use the form of **do** that matches the subject. You can use do as a **main verb** or as a **helping verb**.

  Mom **does** a lot of socializing.

  Mom and I **do** things together sometimes.

  I **do** enjoy chatting with people.

  Mom **does** most of the talking.

  She **does** talk too much at times.

  We **do** try to visit friends and neighbors often.

Present Tense Forms of *Do*
I **do**
he, she, or it **does**
we, you, or they **do**

- The short form of **does not** is **doesn't**. The short form of **do not** is **don't**.

  1. Mom **does not** like the movies.

     Mom **doesn't** like the movies.

  2. We **do not** go to the movies.

     We **don't** go to the movies.

Try It

A. Write do or does to complete each sentence.

1. Dad _____ have a quiet personality.
   do / does

2. My sisters _____, too.
   do / does

3. Mom and I are loud. We _____ have quiet personalities.
   do not / does not

4. She _____ talk loudly.
   do / does

5. I _____ some loud cheering at sports games.
   do / does

6. My brother Ben _____.
   don't / doesn't

7. He _____ act more like Dad.
   do / does

B. Choose words from each column to build five sentences about character traits.

I Mom You Dad He	does doesn't do don't	like busy cities. enjoy big crowds. work hard most of the time. procrastinate a lot. like to hang out with friends.

8. _____

9. _____

10. _____

11. _____

12. _____

Write It

C. Complete the sentences to tell about your personality. Use **do**, **don't**, **does**, or **doesn't** in each sentence.

13. I am like my _____. I _____.

14. I am not like my _____. She _____.

15. I take after my _____. They _____.

16. I do not take after my _____. He _____.

D. (17–20) Imagine you just returned from a family gathering. Write a journal entry to tell what members of your family do and don't like. Use forms of **do** in at least four sentences.

_____

_____

_____

_____

_____

30 Use Verbs to Talk About the Present

Remember: The verbs **be, have,** and **do** each have more than one form in the present. Use the form that goes with the subject.

Forms of *Be*	**Forms of *Have***	**Forms of *Do***
I **am**	I **have**	I **do**
he, she, or it **is**	he, she, or it **has**	he, she, or it **does**
we, you, or they **are**	we, you, or they **have**	we, you, or they **do**

Try It

A. Write the correct form of the verb to complete each sentence.

1. Parents _____ affect their children.
    do / does

2. Each parent _____ an influence.
    have / has

3. My mom _____ like Grandpa in many ways.
    is / are

4. She _____ different in other ways.
    am / is

5. I _____ like and different from both of them.
    am / are

6–7. They _____ teach me a lot, and I _____
    do / does   do / does
    teach them some things, too.

B. Write the correct form of the verb in parentheses to complete each sentence about family influences.

8. Grandpa _____ a piano player. **(be)**

9. He _____ like to share stories of his mother playing the piano. **(do)**

10. All Grandpa's children _____ a love of music. **(have)**

11. They _____ not play the piano, but they play other instruments. **(do)**

12. I _____ a guitar player because I learned to love music from my great-grandparents, my grandparents, and my parents. **(be)**

C. Write sentences to tell how you are like and different from your family. Use a form of **be**, **have**, or **do** in each sentence.

13. My _____ has _____. I _____.

14. My _____ are _____. I _____.

15. My _____ does _____. I _____.

16. My _____ have _____. I _____.

D. (17–20) Who is your oldest relative? Write at least four sentences to tell about that person. Use a form of **be**, **have**, or **do** in each sentence.

_____

_____

_____

_____

_____

Edit It

E. (21–25) Edit this diary entry. Fix five present tense or helping verbs.

July 14

Dear Diary,

Grandpa has his mother's old diary. He are letting me read it. I is surprised at how much my great-grandmother and I has in common. She liked to fish. I does, too. I learned how to fish from Mom. She learned from Grandpa. He must have learned from Great-Grandma! Some things doesn't change at all!

Proofreader's Marks

Change text:

In some ways, families is ~~is~~ are alike.

See all Proofreader's Marks on page ix.

✓ Capitalize the Names of Groups

- Capitalize the main words in the name of a specific organization, government agency, or business.
  Organization: Youth Taking Action
  Government agency: Census Bureau
  Business: Penelope's Boutique
- Do not capitalize **for**, **of**, **and**, and **the**.
  Habitat for Humanity
  Bureau of Labor Statistics
  Aqua Salon and Spa

Try It

A. Use proofreader's marks to correct the capitalization error in each sentence.

1. We are raising money for the Bridge Street dance Company.

2. Sam is working at Florida Department of Environmental protection.

3. The American Red Cross Of Greater New York is having a blood drive.

4. Bella is shopping for the allenville Food Pantry at John's Finer Foods.

5. Did you receive a grant from the Department of Housing And Urban Development?

Proofreader's Marks

Capitalize:
I volunteer at the youngstown animal shelter.

Do not capitalize:
She joined the Girl Scouts Of America.

See all Proofreader's Marks on page ix.

B. Answer each question. Be sure to capitalize the names of groups correctly.

6. What is one of the student organizations at your school?

_____

7. What does it do?

_____

8. If you could work for a specific government agency, which would it be?

_____

✔ Use Semicolons Correctly

- Use a semicolon to join two complete sentences that are closely related. Do not capitalize the first word after the semicolon unless it's a proper noun.

    The fund-raiser was a success; all the guests were having fun.

    Country Catering donated the food; Party City donated the decorations.

- Do not simply use a comma to join two sentences. This causes a **run-on sentence**. So does using nothing at all.

    Incorrect: Everyone wanted to win the raffle, only one person could.

    Correct: Everyone wanted to win the raffle; only one person could.

    Incorrect: Victor bought only one ticket he ended up winning.

    Correct: Victor bought only one ticket; he ended up winning.

Try It

A. Edit each sentence. Add or delete semicolons where necessary.

9. The Student Council has been working hard they've been planning a charity event.

10. They're hosting an all-night bowling party at Rockville Lanes; to raise money for the Rockville Humane Society.

11. Mr. Morton is the faculty supervisor, he is also a volunteer at the Humane Society.

> **Proofreader's Marks**
>
> Add a semicolon:
>
> Some people volunteer⌄ others do not.
>
> Delete:
>
> I volunteer͜ at a soup kitchen.

B. Match each sentence in the first column with a related sentence in the second column. Join them with a semicolon and write each new sentence on the lines.

12. We read about the fund-raiser.   That's very impressive.

13. You raised $1,500.   The other half covered our expenses.

14. Half the money went to charity.   It was in the local paper.

_____

_____

_____

☑ # Check Your Spelling

Homonyms are words that sound alike but have different meanings and spellings. Here are some common homonyms that are often confused with each other.

Homonyms and Their Meanings	**Examples**
to (preposition) = toward	Darrien drove **to** the fund-raiser.
two (adjective) = the number 2	Rhonda won **two** raffle prizes.
too (adverb) = also, more than enough	Corey won a prize, **too**.
	The event was over **too** quickly.
your (adjective) = belonging to you	What is **your** favorite charity?
you're (contraction) = you are	**You're** a good volunteer.

Try It

A. Underline the correct homonym to complete each sentence.

15. We are on our way _____ a fund-raiser at Washington Park.
    to / two / too

16. _____ running in the 5K race, aren't you?
    Your / You're

17. We need to pick up _____ race packets, please.
    to / two / too

B. (18–20) Edit the letter. Fix three homonym errors.
Use proofreader's marks.

Proofreader's Marks

Change text:
                    too
We have ~~to~~ much garbage.
              ∧

Dear Citizens of Edgewater:

Residents Against Garbage Excess (RAGE) is a new organization. It is trying to reduce the amount of garbage that goes two our landfills. In order to stop this problem, we are providing to recycling cans for each family. Every Monday, we will collect all you're recyclables. You're helping save our planet.

Sincerely,

Vicente Alvarez, President

Residents Against Garbage Excess

Name _____ Date _____

Edit and Proofread

✓ Use Subject Pronouns

- Use a **subject pronoun** to replace a noun in the subject of a sentence.

  Lori went to the fund-raising dance. **She** went to the fund-raising dance.
  noun   pronoun

  William and **Patrick** went, too. **They** went, too.
  noun   noun   pronoun

- Use subject pronouns to make your writing less repetitive.

  Lori, **William**, **and Patrick** had a lot of fun at the dance. **They** stayed until the end.

Subject Pronouns	
Singular	**Plural**
I	we
you	you
he, she, it	they

Try It

A. **Add a subject pronoun to complete each pair of sentences.**

21. Students paid to get into the dance. _____ thought of it as a donation.

22. The money went to charity. _____ was donated to the local hospital.

23. Blake and I volunteer at the hospital. _____ bring meals to the patients.

24. Volunteer with us tomorrow. _____ won't be sorry.

B. **(25–30) Replace the underlined <u>nouns</u> with subject pronouns.**

The Kanduns lost their house in a fire. <u>The Kanduns</u> need a new house, but <u>the Kanduns</u> don't have enough insurance money to build one. My friends and I are on the student council. <u>My friends and I</u> are planning a fund-raiser to raise money for the Kanduns. <u>The fund-raiser</u> is going to be a bake sale in the school cafeteria. <u>My friends and I</u> are looking for volunteers to participate. <u>Volunteers</u> can bring baked goods to the cafeteria next Friday morning.

68

© National Geographic Learning, a part of Cengage Learning, Inc.

31 How Do You Show That an Action Already Happened?

Add -ed to the Verb.

- Action in the **present tense** happens now or on a regular basis.
- Action in the **past tense** happened earlier.

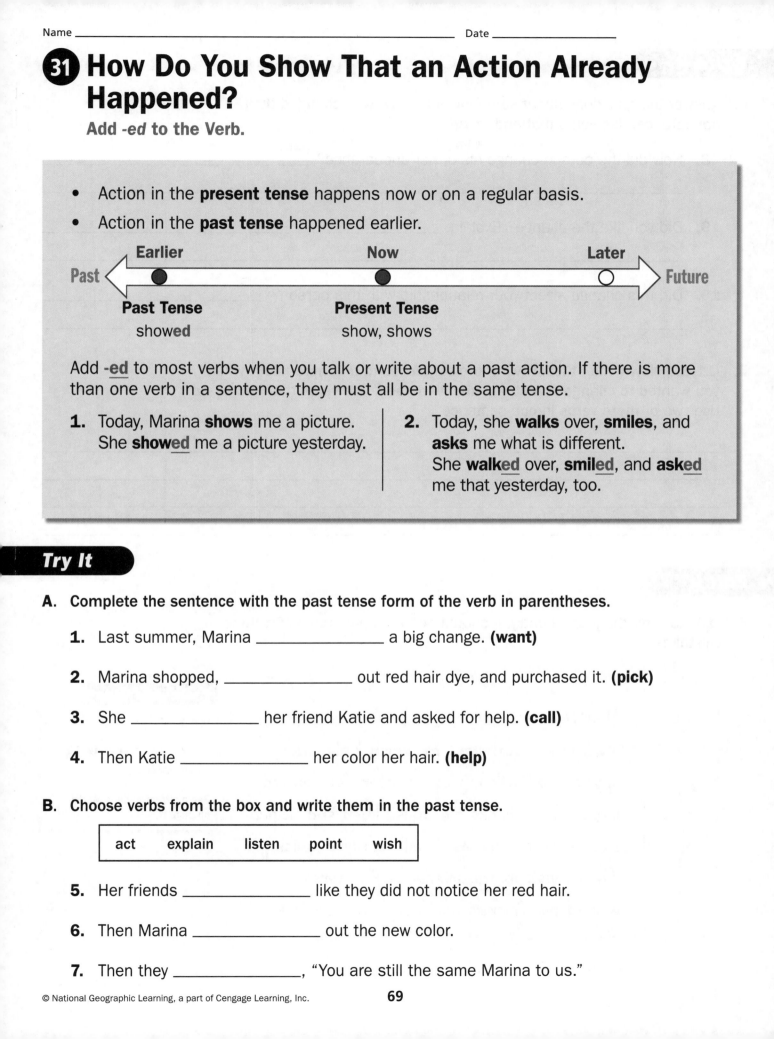

Earlier · Now · Later

Past ← · · · → Future

Past Tense
show**ed**

Present Tense
show, shows

Add **-ed** to most verbs when you talk or write about a past action. If there is more than one verb in a sentence, they must all be in the same tense.

1. Today, Marina **shows** me a picture. She **showed** me a picture yesterday.

2. Today, she **walks** over, **smiles**, and **asks** me what is different. She **walked** over, **smiled**, and **asked** me that yesterday, too.

Try It

A. Complete the sentence with the past tense form of the verb in parentheses.

1. Last summer, Marina _____ a big change. **(want)**

2. Marina shopped, _____ out red hair dye, and purchased it. **(pick)**

3. She _____ her friend Katie and asked for help. **(call)**

4. Then Katie _____ her color her hair. **(help)**

B. Choose verbs from the box and write them in the past tense.

act	explain	listen	point	wish

5. Her friends _____ like they did not notice her red hair.

6. Then Marina _____ out the new color.

7. Then they _____, "You are still the same Marina to us."

C. Answer the questions about someone you know who changed their appearance. Use verbs that end in **-ed**.

8. How did the person change his or her appearance? _____

_____

9. Did you like the change? Explain. _____

_____

10. Did this change affect your relationship with this person? _____

_____

D. (11–12) Now write at least two more sentences to tell more about when you wanted to change something about yourself. Use verbs that end in **-ed**. Use two or more verbs in one sentence.

_____

_____

_____

_____

Edit It

E. (13–15) Edit the journal entry. It should be in the past tense. Fix three mistakes.

May 19

My glasses bothered me when I played sports. So I ask my eye doctor for contact lenses. She checks my eyes. Then she helped me insert the lenses. I walked home quickly. Then I look in the mirror a few times. I wished my friends could see my new look!

Proofreader's Marks

Change text:

The lenses change my appearance.
(changed)

See all Proofreader's Marks on page ix.

© National Geographic Learning, a part of Cengage Learning, Inc.

32 Can You Just Add *-ed* to Form a Verb in the Past?

Not Always

Most verbs end with **-ed** to show the past tense. Sometimes you have to change the spelling of the verb before you add **-ed**. Follow these rules:

1. If a verb ends in silent **e**, drop the **e**. Then add **-ed**.
   Brianna lik**ed** her new haircut. **(like)**
   She hop**ed** James would like it, too. **(hope)**

2. Some one-syllable verbs end in one vowel and one consonant. Double the consonant before you add **-ed**.
   Brianna patt**ed** her hair gently. **(pat)**
   Then she slipp**ed** on her jacket. **(slip)**

Try It

A. **Complete each sentence in the past tense. Use the verb in parentheses.**

1. James _____ on time for their date. **(arrive)**

2. James _____ her new hair style right away. **(notice)**

3. Then Brianna _____ a boutonniere on James's lapel. **(pin)**

4. They both _____. They each liked how the other looked. **(nod)**

B. **Complete the sentences. Choose verbs from the box and write them in the past tense.**

| beg | dance | like | stop |

5. Brianna and James _____ at the party.

6. James _____ dancing and sat by his friends.

7. Brianna _____ her friends to tell her what they thought of James.

8. Her friends _____ James a lot.

Write It

C. Answer the questions about a time you wanted to impress someone. Use verbs with **-ed**.

9. Who did you want to impress? I _____ to impress _____.

10. What did you plan to do? I _____ to _____.

11. How did the person respond to your actions? _____

_____

_____

D. (12–15) Write at least four sentences to tell more about what happened. Use verbs with **-ed**.

_____

_____

_____

_____

Edit It

E. (16–20) Edit the journal. It should be in the past tense. Fix five mistakes.

September 10

Last summer a new girl moved into my
neighborhood. She introduce herself as a
great basketball player. I hope she was joking
because she was very short. One morning
I skip my piano lesson and watched her play.
She dribbles the ball like a pro. She made a
play even when it seemed impossible. I laugh
at my silly ideas. Short people can surely
play basketball!

Proofreader's Marks

Change text:

smiled
She smile at me.

See all Proofreader's Marks on page ix.

72

33 When Do You Use *Was* and *Were*?

When You Tell About the Past

The verb **be** has special forms to tell about the present and the past.

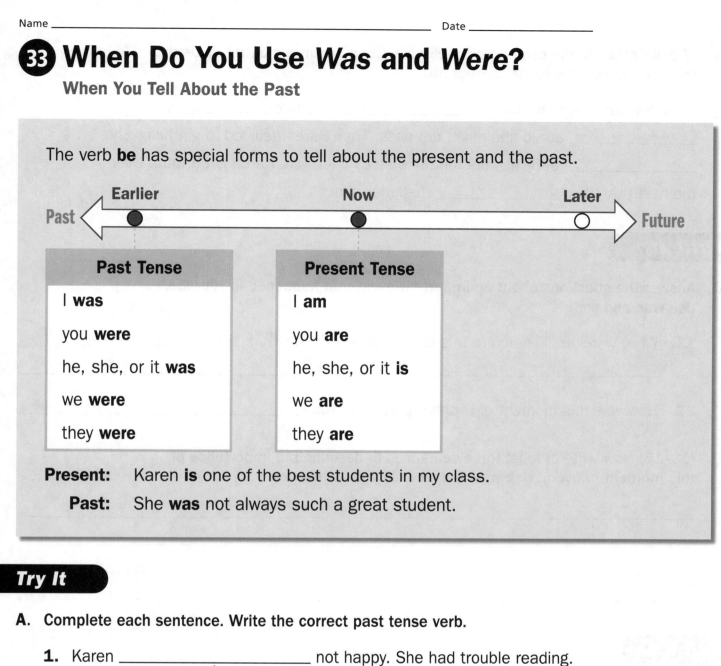

Past Tense	Present Tense
I **was**	I **am**
you **were**	you **are**
he, she, or it **was**	he, she, or it **is**
we **were**	we **are**
they **were**	they **are**

Present: Karen **is** one of the best students in my class.

Past: She **was** not always such a great student.

Try It

A. Complete each sentence. Write the correct past tense verb.

1. Karen _____ not happy. She had trouble reading.
    was / were

2. Her classes _____ important to her.
    are / were

3. Karen _____ happy when she found a good tutor.
    is / was

4. Her tutor _____ very helpful. He taught Karen good reading habits.
    was / were

5. Karen _____ pleased with her progress.
    am / was

6. Her tutor _____ determined to help Karen. Today, she is a great student.
    was / were

B. (7–10) Complete the sentences to tell how Karen became a better student. Use the correct past tense form of **be**.

A few years ago, Karen _____ a poor student. Her teachers _____ afraid she might not pass. Then Karen decided to get help. She _____ ready to work hard and study a lot, too. Karen got a tutor. Over the next year, they _____ together a lot.

Write It

C. Answer the questions about an important event that happened in your life. Use **was** and **were**.

11. What were you like before this event happened? At that time, I _____
_____.

12. How was this moment or event important to you? _____

D. (13–15) Now write at least three sentences to describe the importance of this moment or event. Use **was** and **were** in your sentences.

_____

_____

_____

_____

Edit It

E. (16–20) Edit the letter. It should be in the past tense. Fix five mistakes.

Dear Raul,

    I'm sorry I missed you at the game yesterday. My family and I were at a concert before the game. They are sorry to be late. We was so late, that the game is already over. I am really disappointed. Then I saw you. You are very far away.

Talk to you soon,

Ben

Proofreader's Marks
Change text:
was ℓ He were there.
See all Proofreader's Marks on page ix.

34 When Do You Use *Had*?

When You Tell About the Past

The verb **have** uses special forms to show the present and the past.

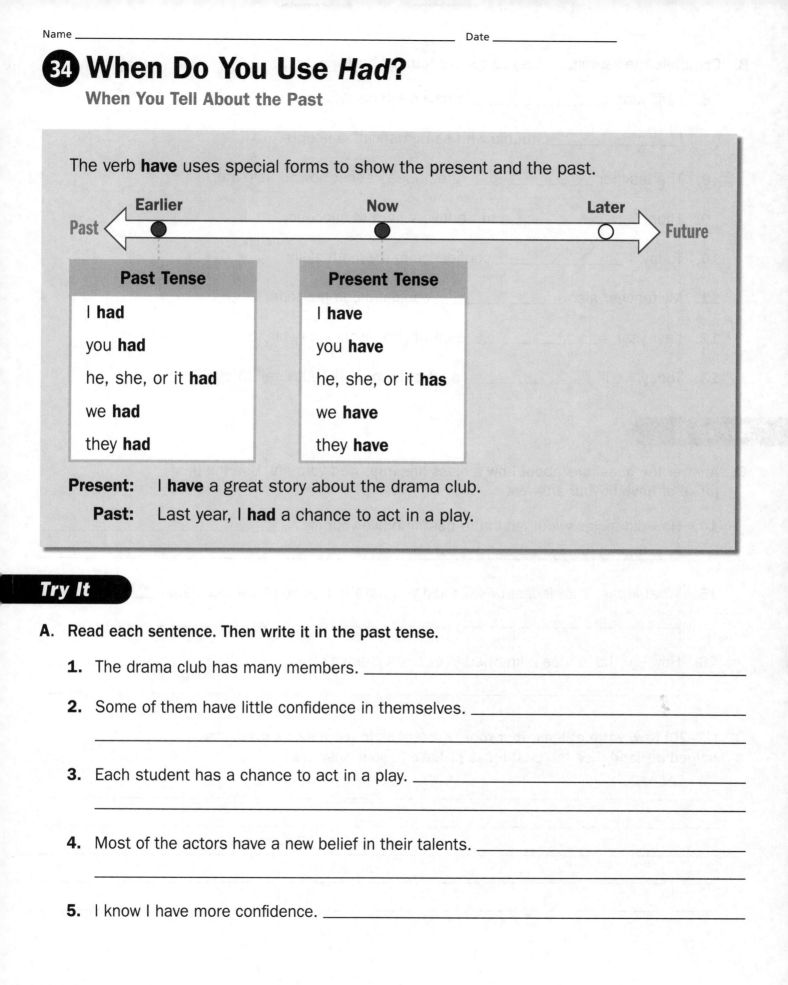

Past Tense
I **had**
you **had**
he, she, or it **had**
we **had**
they **had**

Present Tense
I **have**
you **have**
he, she, or it **has**
we **have**
they **have**

Present: I **have** a great story about the drama club.

Past: Last year, I **had** a chance to act in a play.

Try It

A. Read each sentence. Then write it in the past tense.

1. The drama club has many members. _____

2. Some of them have little confidence in themselves. _____
   _____

3. Each student has a chance to act in a play. _____
   _____

4. Most of the actors have a new belief in their talents. _____
   _____

5. I know I have more confidence. _____

B. Complete the sentence. Use the correct form of have.

6. Last year, I _____ a new math class.

7. I _____ trouble with some difficult concepts.

8. The teacher _____ great ideas about how to help me.

9. Then, I _____ to work very hard to succeed.

10. Today, I _____ confidence in my math skills.

11. My teacher also _____ confidence in me today.

12. Last year, I _____ a lot of homework every night.

13. Today, I still _____ a lot of homework, but I sail through!

Write It

C. Answer the questions about how a class has improved your life. Use the past tense of have in your answers.

14. How did a class you had in the past improve your life? _____

_____

15. What ideas, knowledge, or skills did you have before you took the class? _____

_____

16. How did those ideas, knowledge or skills change? _____

_____

D. (17–20) Now write at least four more sentences to tell about a class that helped a friend. Use the past tense of have in your answers.

_____

_____

_____

_____

_____

35 Use Verb Tenses

Remember: You have to change the verb to show the past tense.
Be sure to use the same tense for all verbs in the same sentence.

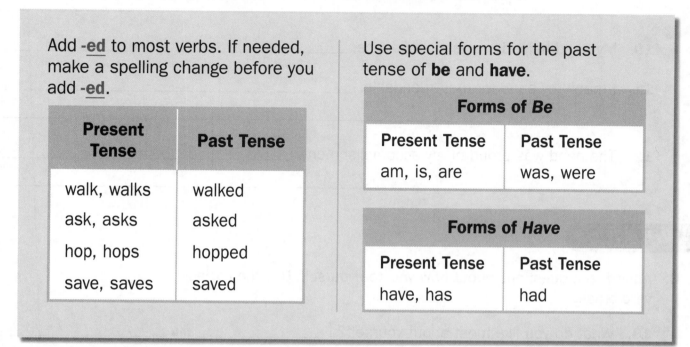

Add **-ed** to most verbs. If needed, make a spelling change before you add **-ed**.

Present Tense	Past Tense
walk, walks	walked
ask, asks	asked
hop, hops	hopped
save, saves	saved

Use special forms for the past tense of **be** and **have**.

Forms of *Be*	
Present Tense	Past Tense
am, is, are	was, were

Forms of *Have*	
Present Tense	Past Tense
have, has	had

Try It

A. Complete each sentence. Write the correct verb.

1. Every Monday, I _____ guitar with my band.
    play / played

2. Last week, I _____ my band with a song that I wrote.
    surprises / surprised

3. I _____ nervous because I didn't think it was very good.
    am / was

4. Then, they _____ me to play the song again.
    ask / asked

5. My heart _____ a beat and I _____ with pride.
    skips / skipped   beam / beamed

6. I _____ up and _____ it again.
    hop / hopped   play / played

7. The band members _____ their heads as they listened.
    nods / nodded

8. I _____ a lesson that day. My band believes in me more than I do.
    learn / learned

B. Read each sentence. Write if it uses present or past tense. Then rewrite the sentence and change the tense.

9. Now I have plans to write many more songs. _____
_____

10. My band helped me gain confidence. _____

11. I thank my band for their friendship. _____
_____

12. The band was proud of my accomplishment. _____
_____

Write It

C. Answer the questions about how you see yourself. Use the correct verb tense.

13. What do you like most about yourself? I _____ my _____.

14. What opinions do your friends have of you? _____
_____

15. Have you changed how you see yourself compared to a year ago? Explain. _____
_____

16. Compare your image of yourself with what your friends think of you. _____
_____

D. (17–20) Now write at least four sentences to tell about things you wish you had changed about yourself. Use the past tense. Use three verbs in at least one sentence. Separate the verbs with commas.

_____
_____
_____
_____
_____

36 How Do You Show That an Action Already Happened?

Change the Verb.

Add **-ed** to most verbs to show that an action already happened. Use special past tense forms for **irregular verbs**.

Present	Past	Example in the Past
do, does	did	Hailey **did** her best on all her science projects.
go, goes	went	Last year, she **went** on a trip to the Science Museum.
get	got	She **got** excellent grades after that.
have, has	had	Last month, her class **had** a science fair.
meet	met	Hailey **met** her science team members.
take	took	She **took** a chance with a new challenge.
tell	told	Hailey **told** her teacher what she wanted to do.

Try It

A. Read each sentence. Write the sentence again, changing the verb to the past tense.

1. Hailey wants to run for leader of her science team. _____

   _____

2. The team tells Hailey she needs to learn new skills. _____

   _____

3. Instead, they take a vote for Ben. _____

4. Ben has great leadership skills. _____

5. The team meets every afternoon for the whole month. _____

   _____

B. Complete the sentences. Choose from the verbs in the box. Use the past tense.

do	get	meet	take	tell

6. Hailey _____ a chance to be part of a real team.

7. Before, Hailey _____ everything by herself.

8. This time, Hailey _____ orders from the team leader.

9. She _____ new friends and team members.

10. Her friends _____ Hailey they like to work with her.

Write It

C. Write three sentences about a time you learned something about yourself from participating in a group. Use the past tense.

11. Tell about what you did. _____

_____

12. Tell about the person or people that you met. _____

_____

13. What did you get from the experience? _____

_____

D. (14–15) Now write at least two more sentences about the experience. Use the past tense.

_____

_____

_____

_____

_____

_____

Name _____ Date _____

37 How Do You Show That an Action Already Happened?

Change the Verb.

Add -<u>ed</u> to most verbs to show that an action already happened.
Use special past tense forms for **irregular verbs**.

Present	Past	Example in the Past
see	saw	Paul **saw** the sign for the class elections.
run	ran	He **ran** right past it on his way to the bus.
sit	sat	Paul **sat** behind Morgan on the bus.
say	said	Morgan **said**, "I think you should run for class treasurer."
feel	felt	Paul **felt** uneasy about the whole thing.
know	knew	He **knew** that it would be hard work.

Try It

A. Complete each sentence. Write the past tense form of the verb in parentheses.

1. Morgan and her friends _____ they would help Paul. **(say)**

2. He _____ he could trust his friends. **(know)**

3. In the end, Paul _____ for class treasurer. **(run)**

4. Everyone _____ Paul's name on the ballot. **(see)**

B. Complete each sentence in the past tense. Write the correct form of the verb.

5. Paul and his friends _____ election posters.
   make / made

6. On election day, the students _____ that it was time to vote.
   know / knew

7. The class advisor _____, "I counted the ballots and Paul is
   says / said
   our new treasurer."

C. Use the questions to help you write about a time you tried something new. Use irregular past tense verbs.

8. What new thing did you try? _____

9. How did you feel about trying it? _____

10. What did you think after you tried it? _____

11. Did you learn something new about yourself? _____

_____

D. (12–14) Write at least three sentences to tell more about when you tried something new. Use irregular past tense verbs.

_____

_____

_____

_____

_____

Edit It

E. (15–20) Edit the letter. Fix six mistakes.

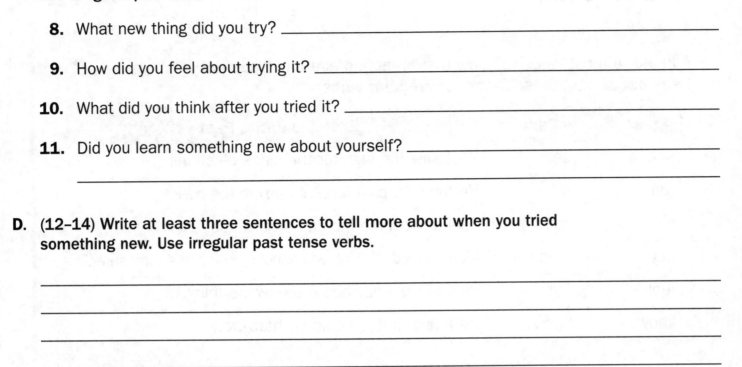

Dear Sonrisa,

   Last month, I ran for class treasurer. At first, I feel nervous. My friends say, "We believe in you." They know I needed them. My friends sit with me on election day. Together, we wait for the final results. Guess what? I won! I make a promise to be a good treasurer.

Your friend,

Paul

Proofreader's Marks

Change text:
                sat
I ~~sit~~ with my friends.
      ^

See all Proofreader's Marks on page ix.

38 How Do You Show That an Action Was In Process?

Use *Was* or *Were* Plus the *-ing* Form of the Verb.

- Sometimes you want to show that an action was happening over a period of time in the past. Use the past progressive form of the verb.

- To form the past progressive, use the helping verb **was** or **were** plus a main verb that ends in **-ing**. The **helping verb** must agree with the subject.

  Liam **was** **running** the school's redecorating project.
  Janice **was** **help**ing him.
  They **were** **tak**ing ideas from different students.

Try It

A. Complete each sentence. Use the past progressive form of the verb in parentheses.

1. Liam _____ for illustrations for the school's halls. **(look)**

2. He _____ for students who like art to participate. **(ask)**

3. The teachers _____ on helping Liam. **(plan)**

4. Liam _____ down all the ideas. **(write)**

5. He _____ a good manager. **(become)**

B. (6–9) Complete the sentence with verbs in the past progressive tense.

6. The teachers _____ their own paintings.

7. Students _____ Liam good ideas about how to hang the art.

8. Liam _____ pride in how he managed the details.

9. He _____ positive about his role in the redecorating project.

C. Describe a project you worked on. Use the past progressive or past tense.

10. Describe what you were doing. _____

_____

11. Tell why you chose this project. What were you hoping to accomplish? _____

_____

12. Describe how you felt at the end of the project. _____

_____

D. (13–15) Now write at least three sentences to tell more about the project. Use the past progressive or past tense.

_____

_____

_____

_____

E. (16–20) Edit the paragraph. Fix five mistakes in the past progressive tense.

One of my favorite projects was a camping trip I organized for my grandfather. I were planning a lot of fun activities. I was hoped we would catch the biggest fish ever. He were wishing for sunny weather. The first night, my grandfather kept me up late. He tell stories about life when he was young. The next night, I kept him up late. I were snoring. Today, we still laugh about this trip.

Proofreader's Marks

Add text:
                was
          ⌃helping my grandfather.

Change text:
      were wishing
We ~~was wishing~~ for a
change. ⌃

See all Proofreader's Marks on page ix.

39 How Do You Tell About the Future?

Use *Will* Before the Verb.

The **future tense** of a verb shows that an action will happen later.

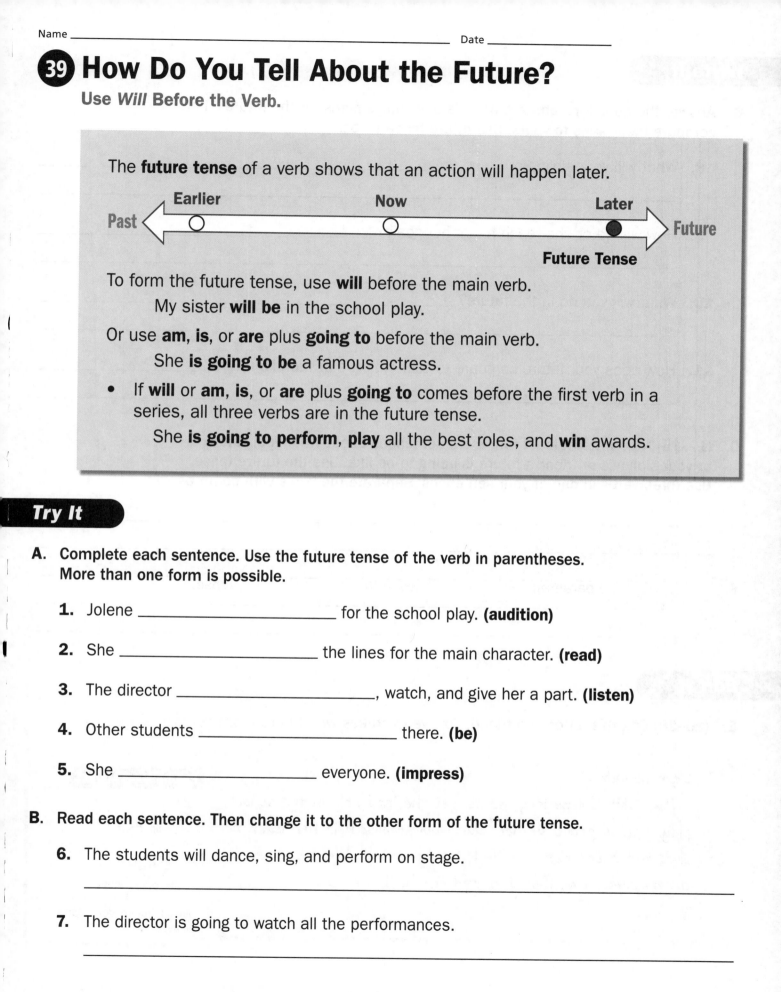

To form the future tense, use **will** before the main verb.

My sister **will be** in the school play.

Or use **am, is,** or **are** plus **going to** before the main verb.

She **is going to be** a famous actress.

- If **will** or **am, is,** or **are** plus **going to** comes before the first verb in a series, all three verbs are in the future tense.

She **is going to perform**, **play** all the best roles, and **win** awards.

Try It

A. Complete each sentence. Use the future tense of the verb in parentheses. More than one form is possible.

1. Jolene _____ for the school play. **(audition)**

2. She _____ the lines for the main character. **(read)**

3. The director _____, watch, and give her a part. **(listen)**

4. Other students _____ there. **(be)**

5. She _____ everyone. **(impress)**

B. Read each sentence. Then change it to the other form of the future tense.

6. The students will dance, sing, and perform on stage.

_____

7. The director is going to watch all the performances.

_____

C. Answer the questions about a friend's or sibling's plans for the future. Then compare their plans to yours. Use future tense verbs.

8. What will your sibling or friend do? _____

_____

9. How will he or she reach his or her goals? _____

_____

10. What will you do in the future? _____

_____

11. How does your future compare to your sibling's or friend's future? _____

_____

D. (12–15) Now write at least four more sentences about what your future or your sibling's or friend's future is going to be like. Use the future tense. Use three verbs in one of your sentences. Separate the verbs with commas.

_____

_____

_____

_____

_____

E. (16–20) Edit this letter to a friend. Fix five mistakes with future tense verbs.

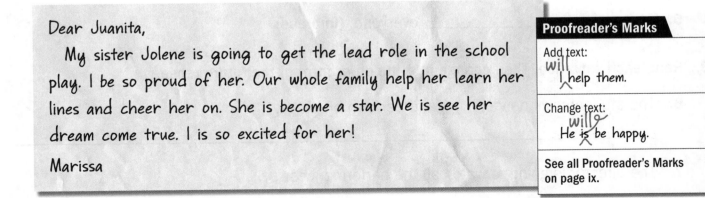

Dear Juanita,

My sister Jolene is going to get the lead role in the school play. I be so proud of her. Our whole family help her learn her lines and cheer her on. She is become a star. We is see her dream come true. I is so excited for her!

Marissa

Proofreader's Marks

Add text:
will
I help them.

Change text:
will
He is be happy.

See all Proofreader's Marks on page ix.

40 Use Verb Tenses

Remember: You have to change the verb to show when an action happens. The action can happen in the **present**, **past**, or **future**.

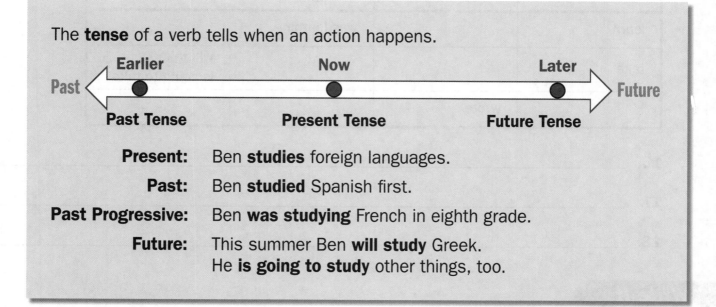

The **tense** of a verb tells when an action happens.

	Earlier	Now	Later	
Past	Past Tense	Present Tense	Future Tense	Future

Present:	Ben **studies** foreign languages.
Past:	Ben **studied** Spanish first.
Past Progressive:	Ben **was studying** French in eighth grade.
Future:	This summer Ben **will study** Greek. He **is going to study** other things, too.

Try It

A. Read each sentence. Write a new sentence. Change each verb to the tense in parentheses.

1. Ben learns Spanish, studies French, and gets A's. **(past)** _____

_____

2. He was taking French lessons, too. **(future)** _____

3. Ben also likes sports. **(past)** _____

4. I see Ben at a tennis match. **(past)** _____

5. Ben played very well. **(past progressive)** _____

6. Ben does many things well. **(past)** _____

7. Ben plays polo, takes golf lessons, and goes horseback riding. **(future)** _____

_____

8. He plays with his friends often. **(past)** _____

B. (9–18) Write the missing forms of each verb in the chart. Then choose verbs from the chart to build three sentences about a friend's accomplishments.

Present	Past	Past Progressive	Future
learn		was learning	
take			will take / is going to take
	wrote		

16. _____

17. _____

18. _____

Write It

C. Use the questions to help you write about your skills. Use three different verb tenses in your sentences.

19. Describe something that you enjoyed doing or were good at in the past. _____

_____

20. How does this activity show the real you? _____

_____

21. Will people be surprised to learn this about you? Explain why or why not. _____

_____

22. Write about something new you plan on learning. _____

_____

D. (23–25) Now write at least three sentences to tell more about ways that you are unique or do not fit a stereotype. Use three verbs in one of your sentences. Separate the verbs with commas.

_____

_____

_____

41 How Do Nouns Work in a Sentence?

They Can Be the Subject or the Object.

- Nouns can be the **subject** of a sentence.
  Bruce is good friends with Dan.
  subject

- Nouns can be the **object** of an action verb. To find the object, turn the verb into a question like: "Play what?" Your answer is the object.
  Bruce and Dan **play baseball**.
  verb   object

- Many English sentences follow this pattern: **subject** → **verb** → **object**.
  Bruce hits the **ball** into the outfield.
  subject verb   object

  Dan wears a **glove** when he is the catcher.
  subject verb   object

Try It

A. Read each sentence. Decide if the underlined noun is a **subject** or an **object**. Write subject or object on the line.

1. The boys both enjoy <u>sports</u>. _____

2. Dan has other <u>interests</u>, too. _____

3. <u>He</u> is an excellent drummer. _____

4. <u>Dan</u> decides to join the jazz band. _____

5. He meets new <u>friends</u>. _____

6. <u>They</u> do not know Bruce. _____

7. But <u>Dan</u> can still be friends with Bruce. _____

8. Dan has his own <u>identity</u>. _____

B. Read each sentence. Write a question that would help you find the object of the sentence.

9. Friends usually have similar interests. _Have what?_ _____

10. They appreciate their differences, too. _____

11. Maybe one friend sings rock music. _____

12. And the other friend writes poetry. _____

13. They can share their special talents. _____

14. Together, they might create a hit song! _____

Write It

C. Write about a good friend of yours. Use the questions to help you talk about your separate identities. Use a subject and an object in each sentence.

15. How did you meet your friend? I met _____

_____.

16. What interests do you and your friend share? We both _____

_____.

17. How are you and your friend different from each other? _____

_____

D. (18–20) Now write at least three more sentences to tell how you and your friend have separate identities. Use a subject and an object in each sentence.

_____

_____

_____

_____

_____

42 Why Are There So Many Pronouns?

Some Work as Subjects, and Some Work as Objects.

- Use a **subject pronoun** as the subject of a sentence.

  Marissa is Tom's sister. **She** rides to school with Tom.　　subject

- Use an **object pronoun** as the object of the verb.

  Tom helps Marissa with her math **homework**. Tom knows how to explain **it**.
  　　object

- Which pronouns stay the same no matter how they are used?

Pronouns	
Subject	**Object**
I	me
you	you
he	him
she	her
it	it

Try It

A. **Read each pair of sentences. Write a pronoun, and underline the noun that it refers to.**

1. Marissa's math teacher remembers Tom. Math was a favorite subject for _____.

2. Math is harder for Marissa. _____ is not her best subject.

3. Marissa admires her brother. She looks up to _____.

4. But Marissa needs a separate identity. Tom wants _____, too.

5. Marissa talks to Tom about it. _____ listens to his advice.

B. **(6–10) Complete each sentence. Write the correct pronoun on the line.**

Marissa tries activities that Tom never did. _____ tries out for the
　　　　　　　　　　　　　　　　　　　　　　　She / Her

track team. The coach asks _____ to join _____. Marissa runs
　　　　　　　　　　　　　she / her　　　　　　　　it / he

well. Before long, people know _____ as an athlete. Marissa creates her
　　　　　　　　　　　　　　she / her

own identity. Tom is happy for Marissa. _____ is proud of her, too.
　　　　　　　　　　　　　　　　　　　Him / He

C. Use the questions to help you write about your unique identity. Use subject and object pronouns correctly.

11. How are you different from other members of your family? I *am* _____

_____.

12. How can you help people see you as an individual? _____

_____

13. What skills or abilities set you apart from others? _____

_____

D. (14–16) Write at least three sentences to tell more about the way you would like others to see you. Use subject and object pronouns correctly.

_____

_____

_____

_____

_____

_____

Edit It

E. (17–20) Edit the scrapbook page. Fix four pronoun mistakes.

That's my brother. He is four years older than me. Him is ten years old in that photo. He is showing I how to ride a bike. Look at this picture of us. Me taught him how to play tennis. Tennis is my favorite sport. My brother doesn't like him as much.

Proofreader's Marks

Change text:

Here is a picture of I.
^ me

See all Proofreader's Marks on page ix.

43 Do You Ever Talk About Yourself?

Then Learn to Use the Words *I* and *Me*.

Subject Pronoun: I

- Use the pronoun **I** as the **subject** of a sentence.

    I am a great dancer.

- In a compound subject, name yourself last.

    Last summer, **Francine and I** tried something new.

    She and I took dance lessons.

- What's wrong with this sentence?

    Me and Francine started with salsa lessons.

Object Pronoun: me

- Use the pronoun **me** as the **object** of a sentence.

    Salsa lessons seemed great for **me**.

- In a compound object, name yourself last.

    Tuesday afternoons were perfect for **Francine and me**.

    The teacher taught **her and me**.

- What's wrong with this sentence?

    The classes helped me and her.

Try It

A. Complete each sentence with **I** or **me**. Write the correct pronoun on the line.

1. The dance teacher showed Francine and _____ each step.
   I / me

2. Francine and _____ practiced one move at a time.
   I / me

3. Soon, _____ wanted to try other dances.
   I / me

4. Ballet interested _____ the most.
   I / me

B. (5–8) Read the conversation. Write **I** or **me** on each line.

A. _____ want to learn to dance. Do you?

B. Yes. But why are you asking _____?

A. You and _____ should take lessons together at Studio 5.

B. Great! When will you take _____?

C. Answer the questions. Use the pronouns I or me.

9. What new activity or sport did you learn or explore with a friend? _____ learned
   _____.

10. How did you and your friend feel about the new activity? _____
    _____

11. How did this new activity change you? _____
    _____

D. (12–15) Now write at least four sentences to tell more about the new activity you explored. Remember to use the pronouns I and me correctly.

_____

_____

_____

_____

_____

Edit It

E. (16–20) Edit the journal entry. Fix five mistakes with pronouns.

April 29

This has been the most exciting week ever
for me! Me and Bryson went white-water
rafting. It was amazing. First, Bryson and me
learned the safety rules. Then, the instructor
taught him and I how to steer the raft. She
took me and Bryson out on the river. Bryson
and me loved every minute of it.

Proofreader's Marks

Change text:

Ben and I̱
M̶e̶ ̶a̶n̶d̶ ̶B̶e̶n̶ went
         ∧
rafting.

See all Proofreader's Marks
on page ix.

(44) Which Pronouns Refer to More Than One?

We, You, They, and *Us, You, Them*

With so many pronouns, how do you know which one
to use in a sentence?

Pronouns	
Subject	**Object**
we	us
you	you
they	them

- Use a **subject pronoun** as the subject.

  My **parents** have big dreams for me. **They** want
  me to follow a certain path.   subject

  My **sister and I** know our parents mean well.
  We appreciate all of their support.
  subject

- Use an **object pronoun** as the object of the verb.

  I have my own **dreams**. My parents don't understand **them**.
  object

  We want to talk to my parents. They agree to talk to **us**.
  subject   object

Try It

A. Complete each sentence. Add a pronoun. Underline the noun or nouns that it refers to.

1. My mom and dad hope I will study education. _____ believe I can be a teacher.

2. My sister and I explain my dreams. _____ tell them how much I want to dance.

3. My parents talk to Renee and me. They argue with _____.

4. Renee talks about dancers. She says, "People enjoy watching _____."

5. My parents say, "Dancers have a difficult life. _____ do not earn
   enough money."

6. I understand what my parents mean. _____ have a good point.

7. Renee and I nod. _____ know our parents have good intentions.

8. But I still have my dreams. I hope my parents will let me pursue _____.

B. Put the words in the right order. Write the new sentence. Make sure pronouns are used correctly.

9. us / parents / can advise _Parents can advise us._

   _____

10. should respect / we / them _____

    _____

11. us / they / want / to be happy _____

    _____

12. still want to please / we / them _____

    _____

13. may surprise / them / our dreams _____

    _____

Write It

C. Answer the questions about your goals. Use subject and object pronouns correctly.

14. What goals do you have for yourself? _____

    _____

15. What are your family's goals for you? _____

    _____

16. How can you and your family better understand each other's goals for your future?

    _____

D. (17–20) Now write at least four more sentences about your goals. Tell how you can convince your family about the value of your goals.

_____

_____

_____

_____

_____

45 Use Subject and Object Pronouns

Remember: Use a subject pronoun as the subject of a sentence. Use an object pronoun as the object of a sentence.

Subject Pronouns	I	you	he	she	it	we	you	they
Object Pronouns	me	you	him	her	it	us	you	them

This year **I** did something new. **It** will be something **I** remember forever. My class took a service trip to Rome City. **We** went there to help hurricane victims. **I** worked very hard to help **them**. **They** were amazing people!

Try It

A. Read each sentence. Replace the underlined word or words with the correct pronoun. Then write the new sentence.

1. My class traveled to Rome City. <u>The city</u> was hit by a hurricane in August.

   _____

2. People went to live in shelters. <u>The shelters</u> were warm and safe.

   _____

3. The children particularly liked Sophie. <u>Sophie</u> dressed as a clown and performed tricks.

   _____

4. Sophie and I helped the adults, too. They thanked <u>Sophie and me</u> for all of our help.

   _____

B. Complete the sentences. Write the correct pronoun on each line.

5. The people treated _____ with kindness.

we / us

6. We enjoyed helping _____ .

they / them

7. One lady told Sophie and _____ her personal story.

I / me

8. She said her experience showed _____ what was important.

she / her

C. Use the questions to help you write about a time you did something new. Use pronouns correctly.

9. What new experience did you have? _____

_____

10. Do you look back at this as a positive experience? Explain why or why not. _____

_____

11. What did you learn about yourself or others from the experience? _____

_____

D. (12–15) Now write at least four sentences to tell more about the outcome of this activity. Use pronouns correctly.

_____

_____

_____

_____

Edit It

E. (16–20) Edit the essay. Fix five mistakes with pronouns.

My classmates and I learned so much in Rome City this week.
Me and my classmates expected to find the city in ruins.
Instead we met warriors. The people survived a great tragedy.
Still, them helped each other. They found joy even in a time
of great sorrow. We went to help they. But in the end, these
warriors helped we. I will always treasure the lessons they
taught me and my friends.

Proofreader's Marks

Change text:
My friend and I
~~Me and my friend~~ went
to help them.

See all Proofreader's Marks on page ix.

✓ Capitalize Quotations Correctly

- Capitalize the first word of a direct quotation that is a complete sentence.

  "**Can** we go inside the store?" asked Jack.

  Mr. Lee replied, "**No**, you are not allowed in the store without an adult."

- Do not capitalize the first word of the second part of a direct quotation when it is a continuation of the sentence.

  "**Then**," said Jack, "**we** will go now."

  "**Say** hi to your dad for me," said Mr. Lee, "**and** ask him to stop by."

Try It

A. **Use proofreader's marks to correct the capitalization error in each sentence.**

1. "good afternoon Mr. Lee," I said.

2. Mr. Lee looked at me and replied, "read the sign, Jack."

3. "It says," Mr. Lee continued, "That no teens or other kids are allowed without an adult."

4. "do you have an adult with you?" he asked.

5. "Teens aren't kids," I explained. "we're adults."

Proofreader's Marks

Capitalize:

"read the sign, Jack," said
≡
Mr. Lee.

Do not capitalize:

"Did you read the sign?"
/He asked.

See all Proofreader's Marks on page ix.

B. **(6–10) Edit the conversation between Jack and his dad. Fix five mistakes.**

I went home to talk to my father. "dad, I don't understand Mr. Lee's rule," I said. "What don't you understand?" He asked.
"well, I don't think it's fair," I explained, "Because teens are not kids. We are adults."
"maybe you need to show him that you are an adult. After all, actions speak louder than words," he said.

✓ Use Quotation Marks Correctly

- Use quotation marks when writing the exact words that a person said.

  Isabel said, "I'm going to the grocery store."

  "Why?" asked Mario. "What do you need there?"

- Do not use quotation marks when describing what a person said.

  Isabel said that she needed flour to make a cake.

- Use a comma before a tag, or words that identify who is quoted. Use a comma after the tag if the sentence continues.

  "I'm going to go with you to the grocery store," said Mario.

  "Hurry up," said Isabel, "because I'm leaving right now."

Try It

A. **Edit each sentence. Add any necessary quotation marks and commas. Delete quotation marks that aren't necessary.**

11. It started to snow so I said that "I would shovel the snow.

12. "Hello Jack," said my friend Karen. What are you doing?"

13. "I'm clearing a path so that people can get in and out of the store" I replied.

14. Mr. Lee came outside and said, "Who told you to do that?

15. You did," I said and smiled broadly. He chuckled and said, "Well, I guess I did."

Proofreader's Marks
Add quotation marks: ᵛActions speak louder than words,ᵛhe replied.
Add a comma: "Let's go‸" said Ali.
Delete: He said ℅that we would be late.℅

B. **Write a sentence as a quotation and a description.**

16. (quotation) _____

17. (description) _____

Name _____ Date _____

✔ Check Your Spelling

Edit and Proofread

- Adding prefixes usually does not change the spelling of the base word.

Prefix	Base Word	New Word
un-	afraid	unafraid
re-	try	retry

- When adding a suffix that begins with a vowel, drop the final **e** from a base word that ends with **e**. If the base word does not end in an **e**, then adding the suffix usually does not change the spelling of the base word.

Base Word	Suffix	New Word
use	-ed or -ing	used or using
learn	-ed or -ing	learned or learning

Try It

A. Write the correct form of the prefix or suffix in each sentence.

18. Jack was angry with Mr. Lee for _____ him leave the store.
    makeing / making

19. Jack _____ to Mr. Lee that he was reliable.
    proveed / proved

20. Before Mr. Lee changed the rule, we were _____ about it.
    unhappy / unnhappy

B. Add the prefix or suffix to the base word to create the new word. Rewrite each sentence.

21. Mr. Lee had to **open** the store later. (**re-**) _____

22. Jack **help** clear the snow in front of the store. (**-ed**) _____
    _____

23. It's **true** that teens cannot be responsible. (**un-**) _____
    _____

© National Geographic Learning, a part of Cengage Learning, Inc.   **101**

✓ Use Correct Verb Tense in Quotations

- Use the past tense of a verb to tell about an action that happened in the past.
  He **told** me to read the sign.
- Do not change the verb tense in directly quoted speech.

Incorrect:	"Actions **spoke** louder than words," he **replied**.
Correct:	"Actions **speak** louder than words," he **replied**.
Incorrect:	"I **was** going to the store," I **told** my dad.
Correct:	"I **am going** to the store," I **told** my dad.

Try It

A. Complete each sentence using the correct verb tense.

24. When I saw the snow piling up in front of Mr. Lee's store, I _____
race / raced
home to grab a shovel.

25. "Where _____ you going?" asked Dad.
are / were

26. "I am going to Mr. Lee's store to help clear a path. The snow _____
is / was
blocking the front door of the store," I replied.

B. (27–30) Edit the conversation between Mr. Lee and Jack. Fix four verb tense mistakes.

"Jack, come here," Mr. Lee said. "I wanted to tell you something."

"What did you want to tell me, Mr. Lee?" I asked.

"I think I was wrong about teenagers. You teach me that teens are responsible. Thank you," he replies, taking down the sign from the door.

Proofreader's Marks

Change text:
                    are
"Teens ~~were~~ not kids,"
I said. ∧

46 How Do I Show Possession?

One Way Is to Use a Possessive Noun.

Use a **possessive noun** to show that someone owns, or possesses, something.

One Owner	Add **'s**.	**Maribel's** friend helped by giving her advice.
More than One Owner	Add **'** if the noun ends in **-s**.	People cannot solve their **friends'** problems for them.
	Add **'s** if the noun does not end in **-s**.	Sometimes **people's** attempts to help are harmful.

Try It

A. Change the underlined words to a phrase with a possessive noun. Write the phrase to complete the sentence.

1. <u>The goal of Maribel</u> _____ is to save more money.

2. <u>Advice from people</u> _____ gives Maribel ideas on how to spend less.

3. One friend tries to change <u>the decisions of Maribel</u> _____.

4. Maribel feels it is not <u>the responsibility of her friend</u> _____.

B. (5–8) Complete each sentence with a possessive noun from the box.

friend's	friends'	people's	person's

Listening to _____ ideas or problems is one way to help people in need. When we listen to a _____ problem, we can give him or her advice. A _____ advice may offer a new point of view. Many people benefit from _____ phone calls or e-mails during difficult times.

C. Answer the questions about your experience helping someone. Use possessive nouns.

9. Describe how you helped solve a friend's or relative's problem. I helped solve my

_____ problem by _____.

10. What were other people's advice to this person? _____

11. What was the person's decision? _____

D. (12–15) What did you think about how other people helped the person you wrote about? Write at least four sentences. Use possessive nouns.

_____

_____

_____

_____

_____

E. (16–20) Edit the advice column. Fix five mistakes in possessive nouns.

Dear Martha:

My best friend, Jane, is funny, kind, and smart. Jane's only flaw is being too dependent on other people. She will not make a decision without asking another persons opinion. She feels more comfortable following teacher's, other student's, or even her little brothers' advice rather than thinking for herself. Janes friends want to help her. How can I help Jane be more independent?

Thanks,

Cindy

Proofreader's Marks
Delete:
My school's teachers are excellent.
Add an apostrophe:
The students work shows progress.
Transpose:
Our teams coach was sick today.
See all Proofreader's Marks on page ix.

47 What's a Possessive Adjective?

It's an Ownership Word.

- Use a **possessive adjective** to tell who has or owns something.

I	→	**my**	I have a friend named Miguel. Miguel is **my** friend.
you	→	**your**	You study hard for exams. **Your** grades are excellent.
he	→	**his**	Miguel works hard. **His** job takes all of his time.
she	→	**her**	Miguel's mother has two jobs. **Her** jobs are both part-time.
it	→	**its**	Miguel's job is hard. **Its** hours are 4:00 to 10:00 at night.
we	→	**our**	We have projects to do. **Our** projects are due this Friday.
they	→	**their**	Some students are finished. **Their** projects are ready.

Try It

A. Complete each sentence about class projects. Write the correct word.

1. _____ friend Miguel asked me for help.
   Me / My

2. He works long hours. He asked me to do _____ project for him.
   he / his

3. My father always says, "Help _____ friends if you can."
   you / your

4. _____ family believes in helping others.
   We / Our

B. Complete each sentence from the author's point of view. Use possessive adjectives **my, your, his, our,** and **their**.

5. I have a close friend. _____ friend needs help.

6. He can't buy _____ lunch because he forgot to ask his parents for money.

7. If _____ friend asked you to give him money for lunch, what would you do?

8. I talked to my parents about it. _____ idea was to remind my friend to ask his parents for lunch money.

9. My family tries to do the right thing. _____ goal is to take care of ourselves but to always help others, too.

Write It

C. Answer these questions about a person you tried to help.
Use possessive adjectives.

10. Whom did you try to help and with what problem? I tried to help _____.

11. How did you try to help? _____

12. How did your help affect the person? _____

13. How did your help enable the person to avoid responsibility? _____

D. (14–17) Now write four sentences about what you learned from trying to help someone. Use possessive adjectives.

_____
_____
_____
_____

Edit It

E. (18–25) Edit the journal entry. Fix eight mistakes.

July 9

I always do my homework on time. Its friend Jane often skips doing hers homework. Sometimes Jane and his friends ask my to do them homework for them. My other friends and I had an idea. We idea was to remind Jane every day to do your homework. Today Jane turned in a lot of work to the teacher. When she handed him the papers, he eyes got big like he was really surprised.

Proofreader's Marks

Change text:

She needs someone to carry she groceries.
her

Delete:

She has trouble climbing hers steps.

See all Proofreader's Marks on page ix.

106

© National Geographic Learning, a part of Cengage Learning, Inc.

㊽ What Are the Possessive Pronouns?

Mine, Yours, His, Hers, Ours, and Theirs

Possessive Adjectives	my	your	his	her	our	their
Possessive Pronouns	mine	yours	his	hers	ours	theirs

Possessive adjectives are used before a **noun**.

Possessive pronouns stand alone.

I feel worried about **my friend** Tanya.	The reaction is **mine**.
Her boyfriend has a temper.	The relationship is **hers**.
His temper makes me nervous.	The temper is **his**.
When he is angry, Tanya and I feel uncomfortable. **Our response** is to be quiet.	The response is **ours**.
Tanya's relatives do not like her boyfriend. **Their hope** is that she will break up with him.	The hope is **theirs**.

Try It

A. Rewrite each sentence. Change the underlined word to the correct possessive pronoun.

1. People say I should not treat Tanya's problem as if it were <u>my</u>. _____

   _____

2. My other friends and I feel that the job of protecting Tanya is <u>we</u>. _____

   _____

3. Other people believe it is up to Tanya and her boyfriend to solve their own problems

   because the relationship is <u>their</u>. _____

   _____

B. Complete each sentence with a verb and a possessive pronoun.

   4. I think my cousin has a problem with overeating. This opinion _____.

   5. You think I should tell my parents. The idea _____.

   6. My cousin thinks he can lose weight easily. He feels the decision _____.

   7. My cousin's parents noticed the problem, too. They feel that the responsibility to support

   my cousin _____.

   8. All our relatives hope he will succeed. The hope _____.

Write It

C. Answer the questions about yourself and your relationships.
Use possessive pronouns.

   9. What types of problems are yours to solve without help from others? Problems that are

   _____ to solve include _____.

   10. How do you feel when friends or relatives think that your problems are theirs to solve?

   When people think my problems are _____ to solve, I feel _____

   _____.

   11. Why should (or shouldn't) people get involved with problems that are not theirs? People

   should get involved with problems that are not _____ when _____

   _____.

D. (12–15) When would you want to help someone with a problem?
Write at least four sentences to explain. Use possessive pronouns.

_____

_____

_____

_____

_____

49 What's a Reflexive Pronoun?

It's a Word for the Same Person.

Reflexive Pronouns			
Singular	myself	yourself	himself/herself/itself
Plural	ourselves	yourselves	themselves

- Use a reflexive pronoun to talk about the same person or thing twice in a sentence. Reflexive pronouns end in **-self** or **-selves**.

  I have a problem at home. **I** cannot solve this problem **myself**.

  My mother does not feel confident.
  She constantly says negative things about **herself**.

  Some people need counseling to develop confidence in **themselves** and their abilities.

Try It

A. Complete each sentence about problems at home. Write the correct reflexive pronoun.

1. Sometimes we have problems at home that we cannot solve _____.
   ourselves / ourself

2. Siblings or parents abuse drugs or alcohol but do not admit it to _____.
   themself / themselves

3. If your caretakers cannot control their anger, you may need help protecting

   _____.
   yourself / yourselves

4. My friend's mother spends too much money and does not have enough left for food for

   _____ or her children.
   himself / herself

5. My neighbor must stop letting his children play alone in the yard because they are too

   young to care for _____.
   themself / themselves

B. Draw a line from each noun or pronoun to the correct reflexive pronoun.

6. Juana   do not know how to care for themselves.

7. The children   has little confidence in herself.

8. We   need help developing confidence in myself.

9. I   know whom to call for help if there is an emergency.

10. You   can control yourself but not anyone else.

Write It

C. Answer the questions about people you know. Use reflexive pronouns.

11. What types of problems at home are too difficult for teenagers to handle themselves?
    Problems that are too difficult for teenagers to handle _____ include
    _____.

12. What can a teenager do to protect herself if she experiences these types of problems?
    To protect _____, a teenager can _____.

13. Whom would you call if you needed to protect yourself? To protect _____, I
    would call _____.

14. Why would you call this person? _____.

15. Have you ever helped a person who could not solve a problem by himself or herself?
    What happened? I helped a boy who couldn't solve a problem by _____.
    He was _____.

D. (16–20) Write at least five sentences about someone who needed your help.
Use reflexive pronouns.

_____

_____

_____

_____

_____

50 Show Possession

Remember: Use possessive words to show that someone owns something. A possessive adjective comes before a noun. A possessive pronoun stands alone.

Possessive Adjectives	my	your	his	her	its	our	your	their
Possessive Pronouns	mine	yours	his	hers		ours	yours	theirs

Try It

A. Complete each sentence. Write the correct possessive word.

1. My uncle is a good person, but he had a problem. _____ problem
   was he couldn't find a job.
   He / His

2. _____ uncle's children had to wear old clothes.
   Me / My

3. My aunt wanted to help. _____ idea was to find "Help Wanted"
   signs in town and give my uncle the addresses.
   His / Her

4. We all helped my uncle in some way. _____ help brought results
   because my uncle found a great job last week.
   We / Our

B. (5–8) Read the paragraph. Complete sentences with either mine, hers, ours, or theirs.

My classmate, Juanita, had a learning disability. This made it difficult for her to take notes. At first I felt the challenge was _____ alone, not _____. However, some other students and I wanted to help. We decided this challenge was also _____. Some students asked the teacher how to help Juanita. The teacher explained that she simply needed notes to study. The students decided to ask a volunteer to take notes for Juanita each day. The idea was really _____, not the teacher's. Every day Juanita took the notes home. She really appreciated the help.

C. Imagine you are one of the students who helped Juanita. Answer the questions. Use possessive adjectives and pronouns.

9. Why did Juanita need your help? She needed _____ help because _____

_____.

10. Whose idea was it to help Juanita? My classmates and I wanted to help Juanita. The idea to help her was _____.

11. How did you help Juanita? We helped by _____.

D. (12–15) Now write at least four sentences describing how a person can encourage others to help themselves. Use possessive adjectives and pronouns.

_____

_____

_____

_____

_____

Edit It

E. (16–20) Edit the journal entry. Fix five mistakes.

August 30

Some people say it is better to let others

help themselves. This is not always true.

Some people just need a little help, and it

isn't his fault. For example, me cousin needed

a little help reading because of its vision. I

helped him read her homework. After he got

glasses, he no longer needed mine help.

Proofreader's Marks

Change text:

How is ~~yours~~ your sister doing? ∧

See all Proofreader's Marks on page ix.

51 What Do Prepositions Do?

Some Show Location.

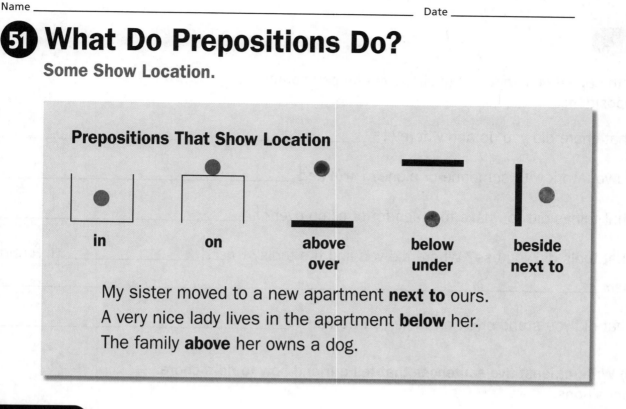

Prepositions That Show Location

| in | on | above over | below under | beside next to |

My sister moved to a new apartment **next to** ours.
A very nice lady lives in the apartment **below** her.
The family **above** her owns a dog.

Try It

A. Complete each sentence about helping a relative move. Add a preposition.

1. We helped my sister pack everything _____ boxes.

2. I packed the dishes. My mother stood _____ me and packed the pots and pans.

3. My father and uncle put a large mat _____ the floor before moving the furniture.

4. They parked the moving truck _____ the alley.

5. When we finished, we rested on the balcony _____ the courtyard.

B. Complete each sentence about helping with a move. Choose the correct preposition.

6. My family moved to be _____ my grandparents.
next to / on

7. We all stood _____ each other, packing different boxes.
beside / over

8. My cousin lived _____ the apartment next to ours.
in / on

9. He helped us carry the boxes _____ the truck.
to / in

10. The sun was high _____ as we drove to our new home.
below / above

**C. Answer the questions about a big chore you helped complete.
Use prepositions.**

11. What chore did you do and where? I _____.

12. Did you work with someone or alone? I *worked* _____.

13. What things did you have to reach for or climb over? I _____.

14. What tools did you use? Where did you find the tools? I *used* _____. *I found*
    them _____.

15. What did you stand or sit on while you worked? _____

**D. (16–20) Write at least five sentences that tell a friend how to do a chore.
Use prepositions.**

_____

_____

_____

_____

_____

Edit It

E. (21–25) Edit the letter. Fix five mistakes.

Dear Arturo,

Thank you for helping me paint my house in the
country. I'm sorry we had to work under such a hot
day. It seemed easier after we put the radio in to us.
The hardest part was painting with the door while
standing in the ladder. You did a great job! Next week,
you can help me paint the trim to the windows.

Max

Proofreader's Marks

Change text:

I live ~~on~~ *in* &Chicago.

See all Proofreader's Marks
on page vi.

52 What Do Prepositions Do?

Some Show Direction.

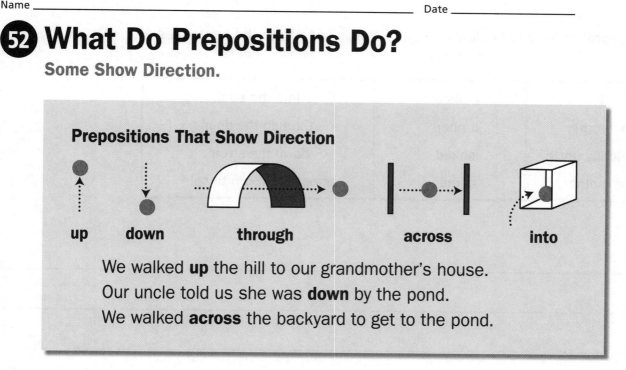

Prepositions That Show Direction

up   down   through   across   into

We walked **up** the hill to our grandmother's house.
Our uncle told us she was **down** by the pond.
We walked **across** the backyard to get to the pond.

Try It

A. Complete each sentence with a preposition that shows direction.

1. My grandmother was very ill. We moved _____ her home to care for her.

2. She lives _____ the street, at the top of the hill.

3. After three days she felt better. We helped her get _____ the stairs.

4. After a week, we took my grandmother on a stroll _____ a park.

5. Then we sat _____ her front porch and rested.

6. After a few minutes, we went back _____ her house.

7. We walked _____ the hall to the living room to talk for awhile.

8. When she felt better, we took her _____ town to visit her friend.

9. We had to pass _____ several neighborhoods before we reached her house.

B. Use the words from each column to build sentences. Write the sentences below.

I	walked	into the pool.
My brother	jumped	through the door.
Our elderly uncle	looked	down the street.
Our mother	came	across the room to help.

10. _____

11. _____

12. _____

13. _____

Write It

C. Answer the questions below about what a sick relative might need. Use prepositions.

14. How can you help a relative who has trouble standing up? I can _____.

15. What things might you bring into the house of an elderly relative? I might bring _____.

16. How can you help a relative if he or she needs to walk down stairs? I can _____.

17. Would you sit across the room or close to your relative? _____

D. (18–20) Now write at least three sentences that suggest how people can care for an elderly relative. Use prepositions.

_____

_____

_____

_____

53 What Do Prepositions Do?

Some Show Time and Origin.

Prepositions That Show Time
- **Time of the day**

    Soccer practice starts **at** three o'clock.
    That is **in** one hour.

- **Days, Months, and Years**

    My father's birthday is **in** January.
    He was born **on** January 30, 1976.

Other Common Prepositions

My parents are **from** England.
We talk to each other **about** our schedules.
We will be gone **from** 8 PM **to** 9 PM tonight.

Try It

A. (1–5) Tell how the family members help each other complete their tasks. Use **about, at, for, from,** or **to.**

In my family, we all help to get chores done before dinner. Dinner is

usually _____ 7 PM. My mother picks up my sister from school at

_____ 3 PM. _____ 4 PM _____ 5 PM each day,

my sister and I do homework. Then _____ a while, my sister and I

clean the house, and my mother fixes dinner.

B. (6–10) Complete each sentence about helping friends. Use **at, for, from, to,**
or **with.**

Friends help each other. _____ school, I did not have any paper.

My friend Daniella gave me several sheets. _____ 11 AM

_____ 12 PM, I ate lunch _____ my friends. Mariellen

had nothing _____ lunch. She left hers at home. We each gave her

something. Then she had plenty to eat!

C. Answer the questions about someone who helps you. Use prepositions.

11. At what times of the day do you usually need help? I *need help* _____.

12. Who can you always go to for help? I *can always go* _____.

13. Do you talk with this person when you don't need help? _____

14. What do you talk about? _____

15. When do you usually see this person? _____

D. (16–18) Now write at least three sentences about friends you help and who help you. Use prepositions.

_____

_____

_____

E. (19–25) Edit the journal entry. Fix seven mistakes in prepositions.

May 19

I had a terrible day, but I realized how lucky I am. First, I got to school in 9 AM (very late on the morning). The teacher was already talking for the class. When I sat down, I fell around my chair. Later, I was walking with the lunch line to my table, and I dropped my lunch tray at the floor. Three friends helped me clean up the mess. Luckily, in friends are always there when I need them.

Proofreader's Marks

Change text:

My birthday is ~~on~~ *in* March.

See all Proofreader's Marks on page ix.

Name _____   Date _____

54 How Do I Know It's a Prepositional Phrase?
Look for the Preposition.

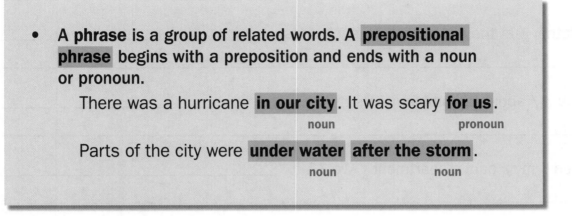

- A **phrase** is a group of related words. A **prepositional phrase** begins with a preposition and ends with a noun or pronoun.

   There was a hurricane **in our city**. It was scary **for us**.
   noun   pronoun

   Parts of the city were **under water after the storm**.
   noun   noun

Try It

A. Complete each sentence about helping a family during an emergency. Choose the correct prepositional phrase.

around the city	to everyone	into my grandparents' house
after the storm	with my grandparents	under the attic
for her help	at the old desk	in the afternoon

1. We needed help _____.

2. The amount of damage the storm did was surprising _____.

3. My parents and I moved _____.

4. After the hurricane, we could not walk _____ because of the flood.

5. Our house was flooded, so we lived _____ for four months.

6. My brother and I had a small room _____.

7. We helped my grandmother make dinner _____.

8. We did our homework _____.

9. We thanked my grandmother _____.

© National Geographic Learning, a part of Cengage Learning, Inc.   119

B. Use the words to form sentences that describe a family in need of help.

10. Our family / an emergency / in April / had _____

_____

11. My father / at the car factory / his job / lost _____

_____

12. my aunt / about the problem / He told _____

_____

13. moved / my / aunt's apartment / We / into _____

_____

14. father / a new job / My / an/ office / in / found _____

_____

Write It

C. Answer the questions about situations when families need help. Use prepositional phrases.

15. What types of problems might families have about money? Families _____.

16. Where can families go for help with these problems? They can _____.

17. What are challenges in living with another family during an emergency? _____

18. What are other ways to help people after an emergency? _____

D. (19–20) Now write at least two sentences that tell more about helping people during an emergency. Use prepositional phrases.

_____

_____

_____

_____

_____

55 Use Prepositions Correctly

Remember: Use prepositions to add details to your sentences.

- Add a prepositional phrase to tell where or when.
  My sister received her diploma.
  My sister received her diploma **in the high school auditorium**.
  My sister received her diploma **on Friday**.
- A prepositional phrase can also show direction.
  My relatives drove **across the state** to attend the graduation.

Try It

A. Add a preposition to complete each sentence. Choose a preposition from the box.

at	in	to	up

1. My cousins did not attend the graduation because they were _____ school.

2. My aunt and uncle got _____ the high school an hour early.

3. We reached the auditorium _____ 10 AM. We were on time for the ceremony.

4. My parents smiled when my sister walked _____ the stairs onto the stage.

5. We had a big party for my sister _____ the evening.

B. (6–10) Read the invitation to a wedding. Add a prepositional phrase to complete each sentence. Choose a preposition from the box.

at	down	in	on	through

You are invited to attend our wedding. It will take place _____.
It will begin _____. Find the address on the enclosed card. When
you reach the church, walk _____. Then go _____
in back. The ceremony will take place _____.

C. **Answer the questions about an important family event you attended. Use prepositional phrases.**

11. When was the event held? The event was held _____.

12. Where was the event? The event was _____.

13. How long did the event last? It lasted _____.

14. What types of things did you see next to and around you? _____

_____

15. Who else came to the event? _____

D. **(16–20) Now, write at least five sentences that describe more about the family event you attended. Use prepositional phrases.**

_____

_____

_____

_____

_____

Edit It

E. **(21–25) Edit the letter. Fix five mistakes in prepositions.**

Dear Linda,

Thank you for coming to my baby shower for
Thursday. I hope it was easy into you to come at the
evening! I know you drove on town to come. It was fun
sitting next you. Most of all, thank you for the beautiful gift.
Sincerely,
Kim

Proofreader's Marks
Add text: The wedding was 1 PM. *(at inserted before 1)*
Change text: We went to a party for Sunday. *(for changed to on)*
See all Proofreader's Marks on page ix.

56 Can I Use a Pronoun After a Preposition?

Yes, Use an Object Pronoun.

- Use an **object pronoun** after a **preposition**.

  My cousin was injured. We take care **of him**.
  We do a lot **for him**.

Object Pronouns	
Singular	**Plural**
me	us
you	you
him, her, it	them

Try It

A. Complete each sentence about people who need special care. Add an object pronoun after the preposition.

1. My cousin injured his legs in an accident. We care for _____ in many ways.

2. When my cousin needs help, he is not afraid to ask for _____.

3. We visit my cousin often. He enjoys spending time with _____.

4. My cousin has a baby daughter. Sometimes we help him take care of _____.

5. My cousin is a strong person. It is a joy to spend time with _____.

B. Complete each sentence about someone who needs special care. Write the correct object pronoun.

6. My neighbor is blind. His hearing is very important to _____.

it / him

7. He is comfortable in our neighborhood. He walks around _____ daily.

them / it

8. My neighbor needs to hear sounds very clearly. It is important for

   _____ to help him by being close.

me / you

9. My neighbor's children and grandchildren visit him often. He loves to sit and talk with

   _____.

it / them

C. Answer the questions about a person who needs to be cared for. Use prepositional phrases with pronouns.

10. Who do you know who needs special care? _____

11. What do people do for him or her? _____

12. Who visits him or her? _____

13. What could you do for him or her? _____

14. What does this person's experience mean to you? _____

D. (15–19) Now write at least five sentences about this person, using prepositional phrases and pronoun objects.

_____

_____

_____

_____

_____

Edit It

E. (20–25) Edit the journal entry. Fix six mistakes.

July 23

My brother needs special care from us. He is a baby, so we must take care of her. Babies can harm themselves easily, so someone must always stay with they. My brother needs lots of attention, so it is important for them to play with he. He loves listening to people and looking at they. I love taking care of my brother. It is always fun for I.

Proofreader's Marks

Change text:

I handed the message to ~~she~~ her.

See all Proofreader's Marks on page ix.

57 In a Prepositional Phrase, Where Does the Pronoun Go?

It Goes Last.

- A **prepositional phrase** starts with a preposition and ends with a noun or pronoun. Sometimes, it ends with both. Put the pronoun last.

  Last week my friend Sarah got crutches. She taught a lesson **to my sister and me**.

- Avoid these common mistakes in a prepositional phrase:

  1. Use **me**, not **I**: Sarah explained to my sister and ~~I~~ me, that she broke her leg.

  2. Put **me** last: Sarah seemed calm to ~~me and my sister.~~ my sister and me

Try It

A. Complete each sentence about a person who prevails over a disability. Write the correct pronoun.

1. My father drives us to school each day. I ride in the car with my sister and
   _____.
   he / him

2. Sarah and her brother Tom walk to school. Their parents cannot provide a ride for Sarah and _____.
   her / him

3. My sister and I sometimes see Sarah with Tom and other students in the mornings. We wave at Sarah and _____ when we pass.
   they / them

4. Sarah broke her leg, and she began to use crutches. This made the walk to school very difficult for Tom and _____, but they never complained.
   she / her

5. My father and I invited Sarah and Tom to ride with _____. It is fun to have everyone in the car together.
   them / us

B. (6–12) Complete each sentence about a person meeting a challenge. Use **me**, **him**, **us**, or **them**.

I never knew a deaf person until I met Roberto. Roberto is a good friend to my brother Misha and _____. I am around Misha and _____ almost every day. We play video games together. It is fun for _____ and _____. Roberto usually wins. He and Misha play baseball with teammates. Misha likes to play baseball with Roberto and _____. Roberto is the star pitcher. After the games, Roberto makes dinner for my brother and _____. Misha clears the table, and Roberto helps _____. Roberto is a great teammate and a kind friend.

Write It

C. Answer the questions below about what a sick relative might need. Use prepositions and object pronouns.

13. Whom have you known who has overcome a disability? _____

_____

14. What activities are challenging for this person? _____

_____

15. What is the difference between how this person and other people view challenges?

_____

D. (16–20) Now write five sentences that tell more about the way this person overcomes challenges and inspires others. Use prepositional phrases with pronouns.

_____

_____

_____

_____

_____

Name _____ Date _____

58 What's an "Antecedent"?

It's the Word a Pronoun Refers To.

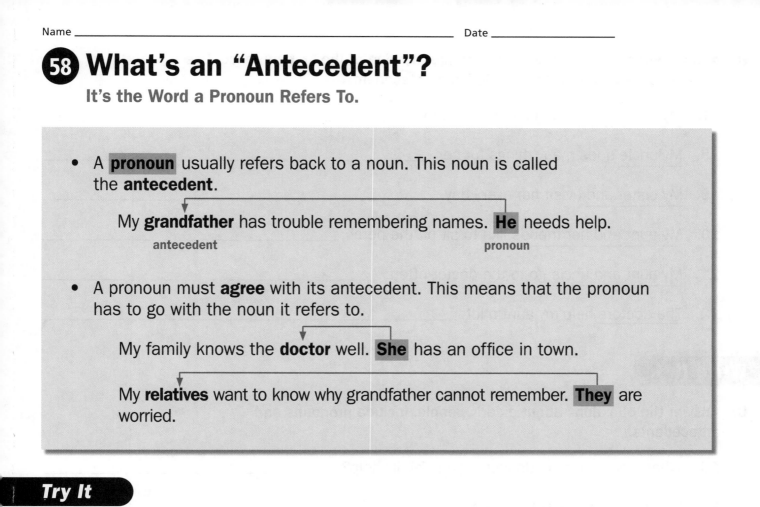

- A **pronoun** usually refers back to a noun. This noun is called the **antecedent**.

  My **grandfather** has trouble remembering names. **He** needs help.
  antecedent   pronoun

- A pronoun must **agree** with its antecedent. This means that the pronoun has to go with the noun it refers to.

  My family knows the **doctor** well. **She** has an office in town.

  My **relatives** want to know why grandfather cannot remember. **They** are worried.

Try It

A. Identify the antecedent for the underlined pronoun. Add a sentence using the pronoun.

1. My grandfather needs to take medicine. He has trouble remembering. _____
   _____

2. My parents and I help grandfather each day. We check that he takes his medicine.
   _____

3. Exercise will help grandfather remain alert. It is also important for his physical health.
   _____

4. My aunt takes grandfather on a walk around the block. She does it every day.
   _____

5. My cousins visit grandfather often. They play chess with him. _____
   _____

6. My sister explains things when grandfather feels confused. She is patient.
   _____

© National Geographic Learning, a part of Cengage Learning, Inc.   **127**

B. Add a sentence to each item to continue the idea of the first sentence. Use the correct pronoun for each underlined antecedent.

7. My elderly aunt has pain from arthritis. _____

8. My uncle does many things for her. _____

9. My sister and I visit her every day. _____

10. My aunt and her friends like to sit on the porch. _____

11. My aunt and uncle go to the doctor often. _____

12. The doctors help my aunt a lot. _____

Write It

C. Answer the questions about elderly people. Include pronouns and antecedents.

13. What elderly person do you or your family help? _____

14. Why does this person need help? _____

15. In what ways does each family member help this person? _____

_____

16. How does this person view help from others? _____

_____

17. What other activities does this person like to do? _____

_____

D. (18–20) Now write at least three sentences about an elderly person in need of help. Use the correct pronoun for each antecedent.

_____

_____

_____

_____

59 How Do I Make Possessive Adjectives Agree?

Match Them to the Noun.

Possessive adjectives usually refer back to a noun. If you're not sure which possessive adjective to use, first find the antecedent, the noun it refers to. Ask yourself:

- Does the antecedent name a man or a woman?
  Use **his** for a man and **her** for a woman.
  A **man** set up this shelter for the homeless. **His** name is Marco.
  One **woman** there was very thin. **Her** children looked healthy.

- Does the antecedent name one or more than one?
  The **people** in line were polite and quiet. They ate **their** food quickly.

Try It

A. Complete each sentence about services in a homeless shelter. Add a possessive adjective that matches the underlined noun in the first sentence.

1. <u>Marco</u> runs the shelter. _____ goal is to keep people off the streets.

2. <u>Homeless people</u> are thankful for the shelter. _____ lives are difficult.

3. <u>Some people</u> volunteer at the shelter. Marco appreciates _____ help.

4. <u>One homeless lady</u> comes every day. She lost _____ job a year ago.

5. <u>The man</u> behind her in line has a mental disability. _____ friends helped him find this shelter.

B. Complete each sentence with a possessive adjective.

6. A father brought his wife and child to the shelter. _____ child laughed and played as she ate.

7. The man's name is Joe. _____ wife is Clara.

8. They visit the shelter because they lost _____ home in a fire.

9. They are thankful to have a place to sleep. _____ room is warm.

Write It

C. Answer the questions about homeless shelters. Use possessive adjectives correctly.

10. How is the life of a homeless family different from the lives of others? _____

_____

11. How can a shelter help a homeless person? _____

12. What needs does a homeless person have trouble getting? _____

13. How can a shelter help a homeless family? _____

14. How do you think a homeless person feels about places that offer free food and

shelter? _____

D. (15–18) Write your thoughts about homeless shelters. Write at least four sentences.

_____

_____

_____

_____

Edit It

E. (19–25) Edit the journal. Fix seven mistakes.

October 15

I saw a homeless man. He pushed her belongings
in a cart. People passed he, but many kept her
eyes straight ahead. I passed him, too. I wallet
was empty. The man stopped to ask a woman a
question. She face looked afraid until he asked
the time. He voice sounded rough and tired.
I wonder if homeless people have families. Do
they families know they are homeless?

Proofreader's Marks

Change text:

The woman comes every
day to the shelter for
~~his~~ here evening meal.

See all Proofreader's Marks
on page ix.

60 Use the Correct Pronoun

Remember: When you use a pronoun, be sure it fits correctly into the sentence. Also be sure it goes with the noun it refers to.

- Use a **subject pronoun** in the subject of a sentence. Use an **object pronoun** after the verb or after a preposition.

  This **camp** is for **adults** with special needs. **It** is fun for **them**.

  The **volunteers** helped **Nancy** finish her project. **They** helped **her** with the instructions.

- All **pronouns** must agree with the **noun** they refer to. This noun is called the antecedent.
  1. If the noun names a male, use **he** or **him**.
  2. If the noun names a female, use **she** or **her**.
  3. If a noun names one thing, use **it** or **it**.
  4. If a noun names "more than one," use **they** or **them**.

Try It

A. **(1–5) Complete each sentence about the camp. Write the correct subject and object pronouns.**

A lady from my neighborhood attended the camp. _____

She / He

really liked it. My friend volunteered with adults at the camp. He worked on

many activities with _____. The adults at the camp

they / them

learned new songs. _____ sang the songs while I played

They / Them

the guitar. One lady at the camp gave each volunteer a wooden picture frame.

_____ made them by hand! The volunteers were sad to say

She / Her

goodbye to the adults at camp. We hugged _____ before

them / they

we left.

B. (6–9) Complete the paragraph about a class for adults with special needs. Use **it**, **them**, or **they**. You can use some pronouns more than once.

Our institute is holding a semester-long class for adults with special needs. _____ will help _____ with daily tasks, such as using a computer. Several qualified instructors will teach a new skill each week. _____ will teach _____ by modeling how to do things.

Write It

C. Imagine a class or event that helps people learn important skills. Answer these questions about it. Use prepositional phrases.

10. What type of class or event is it? _____

11. Who is the class for? _____

12. Who teaches or leads the class? _____

D. (13–15) Now write at least three sentences that describe more about the class or event. Use subject and object prepositions.

_____

_____

_____

Edit It

E. (16–20) Edit the journal. Fix five mistakes in pronouns.

March 28

Today my track teammates won an award at camp. Nina uses a prosthetic, or artificial, leg. She is on the track team with they. My teammates are grateful to she because it runs fast. The medals are a victory for Nina and they. Them are all very proud.

Proofreader's Marks

Change text:

The race began early for the other team and ~~we.~~ us

See all Proofreader's Marks on page ix.

132

© National Geographic Learning, a part of Cengage Learning, Inc.

✓ Capitalize the Names of Places

- Capitalize all main words in the names of specific places such as countries, cities, states, and buildings. Do not capitalize **the**, **and**, or **of**.
  Country: United States of America
  City and State: Miami, Florida
  Building: Empire State Building
- Do not capitalize the names of nonspecific places.
  a country
  a city or state
  a building

Try It

A. (1–8) Fix eight capitalization errors in the letter. Use proofreader's marks.

Dear Parents and Students:

This year's senior class trip destination is chicago, illinois. We will leave on Friday, May 30 and return the following Sunday. Students and parent chaperones will stay at the comfort inn near the sears tower. Students will be able to tour the City and learn about the architecture of its Buildings. Students who are interested in the trip should plan to attend a meeting on Tuesday, March 11.

Sincerely,

Duane Edwards, Principal

Proofreader's Marks

Capitalize:

We went to charlotte, north carolina on our trip.

Do not capitalize:

We saw a football game at Bank Of America Stadium.

See all Proofreader's Marks on page ix.

B. Answer each question. Be sure to capitalize the names of places correctly.

9. What is the last city you visited? In what state was it located?

_____

10. What is the tallest building in your city or town?

_____

✓ Use Apostrophes Correctly

- Use an apostrophe to represent a missing letter or letters in a contraction.
   Our school does**n't** tolerate bullying.

- Use an apostrophe with the letter **s** to show possession.
   You must obey the school**'s** policy.

- Do not add the letter **s** to a plural word to show possession. The apostrophe goes after the final **s** of the word.
   Does the girls**'** school have a similar rule?

- Do not use an apostrophe with the possessive form of **it**. Do use an apostrophe with the contraction **it is**.
   Its rule is the same.
   It's good that schools are taking action against bullying.

Try It

A. Edit each sentence. Add or delete apostrophes where necessary.

11. A speakers presentation is on the consequences of bullying.

12. The principal hopes all the student's questions will be raised.

13. Its important that students join the fight against bullying.

14. They need to recognize it's causes.

B. (15–18) Edit the journal entry. Replace the underlined words with a contraction or possessive form.

Proofreader's Marks
Add an apostrophe:
It͝s not fun being the victim of a bully.
Delete:
The school needs to change it̶'̶s policy.

I <u>am</u> really nervous about starting at my new school. <u>It is</u> hard to transfer in as a sophomore. I hope <u>the attitudes of the other students</u> are friendly and positive. I hope <u>they will</u> become my friends.

✔ Check Your Spelling

- Add **-es** to nouns that end with the letters **ch**, **s**, **sh**, **x**, and **z** to make them plural.
  Stephanie brought her **lunch**. We're buying our **lunches**.
  Richard only takes one **bus** to get to school. Alex takes two **buses**.
  Olivia saw one **flash** of lightning. I saw at least four **flashes**.
  Brooke fit all her belongings in one **box**. Chad needed three **boxes**.
- If a noun ends in a consonant + **y**, change the **y** to **i** and then add **-es**.
  Our school used to have one **bully**. Now it has several **bullies**.
- For some nouns that end in **f** or **fe**, change the **f** or **fe** to **v** and then add **-es**.
  Shelby ate one **half** of her sandwich. Tony ate both **halves**.
  I ran for my **life**. They ran for their **lives**.

Try It

A. Complete each sentence with the plural form of the noun in parentheses.

19. Krystal and Justine used to be _____. **(enemy)**

20. They often played mean _____ on each other. **(hoax)**

21. One day, Krystal's purse was stolen by _____. **(thief)**

22. Justine heard her _____ and came to her aid. **(cry)**

23. From then on, they only had good hopes and _____ for each other. **(wish)**

B. (24–26) Edit the memo. Fix three spelling errors. Use proofreader's marks.

To: All Teachers
From: Principal Juarez
This is a reminder that we will not tolerate bullys on campus.
They disrupt our classs and interfere with learning processes.
If you catch a student bullying another student, stop it
immediately. Do not accept any apologys from the bully. Send
him or her directly to my office.

Proofreader's Marks
Change text:
I don't like ~~bullys~~. bullies

✓ Use Possessive Adjectives

- Use a **possessive adjective** before a noun to show possession.

  Marcus is upset. **His** brother was the target of a bully.

  Angela is upset, too. **Her** brother is the bully.

- Do not confuse the possessive adjectives **your**, **its**, and **their** with the contractions **you're**, **it's**, and **they're**.

  What happened to **your** locker? **You're** having trouble opening it.

  It's jammed. I can't open **its** door.

  They're strong. They can use **their** strength to force it open.

Possessive Adjectives	
Singular	**Plural**
my	our
your	your
his, her, its	their

Try It

A. Use the correct possessive adjective or contraction to complete each sentence.

27. If _____ being bullied, you can protect yourself.

your / you're

28. Most adults will do everything in _____ power to help you.

their / they're

29. Stay with _____ friends and you won't be an easy target.

your / you're

30. If _____ safe, try to stand up to the bully.

its / it's

B. (31–35) Complete the paragraph by adding possessive adjectives and contractions.

We must stop bullying. It's the only way to protect _____ students. Victims of bullying are affected well into _____ adult lives. _____ also at risk of becoming bullies themselves. The school needs to change _____ policy on bullying and practice "zero tolerance." Parents, you need to talk to _____ children about bullying. Together we can make a difference.

61 What Are Adjectives?

They Are Describing Words.

- You can describe people, places, or things with **adjectives** . They answer the question: What is it like?
- Use adjectives to describe:
  1. how something looks: **short, large, blue, beautiful**
  2. how something sounds: **loud, buzzing, noisy**
  3. how something feels, tastes, or smells: **smooth, sweet, moldy**
  4. a person's mood: **friendly, confident, frightened, brave**
- Adjectives help the reader visualize what you are writing about.
  Drew saw the **tall** boy looking at his **new** jacket.
  The **tough** boy gave Drew a **cold** smile.

Try It

A. **Complete each sentence with an adjective from the box.**

blue	hard	loud	metal	unblinking

1. The boy said he wanted Drew's _____ jacket.

2. He gave Drew a _____ shove.

3. Drew stared at the boy with _____ eyes.

4. Drew pulled up the jacket's _____ zipper.

5. He spoke to the boy in a _____ voice.

B. **(6–13) Add adjectives to give a clearer picture.**

The new boy walked into the _____ cafeteria. The school bully

yelled _____ things at him. Then a _____ girl gave the new

boy a _____ smile. The _____ boy took _____

steps and sat down at a _____ table with his _____ friends.

Write It

C. Answer the questions about bullies. Use adjectives in your answers.

14. What is a bully? A bully is _____ who _____.

15. What do bullies do to get their way? Bullies use _____ to _____.

16. How do you feel when a bully bothers you? _____

17. What is the best way to deal with a bully? _____

_____

D. (18–20) Now write at least three sentences to tell how to act confidently toward a bully. Use adjectives in your sentences.

_____

_____

_____

_____

_____

Edit It

E. (21–25) Improve the journal entry. Add five adjectives to make it more interesting.

March 10

I learned an important lesson today. I won't let bullies bother me. I will use my voice and walk with steps. I can find a solution. I have a lot of friends. No one will bully a kid like me!

Proofreader's Marks

Add text:

He wore a jacket. (shiny)

See all Proofreader's Marks on page ix.

138 © National Geographic Learning, a part of Cengage Learning, Inc.

62 Where Do Adjectives Appear in a Sentence?
Usually Before the Noun

- Often the **adjective** comes before the **noun** you are describing.
  On the **first day** of school there was a **warm breeze**.
  Toni wore a **red band** in her **curly hair**.

- If two adjectives both describe the noun, separate them with a comma (,).
  She had **shiny, beaded earrings**.
  Toni also had a **big, bright smile**.

Try It

A. Tell what happens in the story about Toni. Add an adjective to each sentence.

1. Toni knew this would be a _____ school year.

2. Last year, Alex made _____ noises at her in the halls.

3. But now Toni had a _____ plan.

4. She opened the _____, _____ doors.

5. Alex gave her an _____ look.

B. Add details to the story. Choose from the adjectives in the box.

| brown | calm | confident | hateful | loyal |

6. Toni gave Alex a _____ smile.

7. Alex said some _____ words.

8. Toni looked right at him with her _____ eyes.

9. She spoke to Alex in a _____ voice.

10. Then Toni walked over to her _____ friends.

C. Answer the questions about Toni and Alex. Use adjectives in your answers.

11. What do you think Alex will do now? Alex will _____

_____.

12. What action do you think Toni should take then? _____

_____

13. What else can Toni do if Alex bothers her? _____

_____

D. (14–15) Now write at least two sentences to describe how you look and act when you feel confident. Use adjectives in your sentences.

_____

_____

_____

_____

_____

Edit It

E. (16–20) Edit the letter. Put five adjectives in the right place.

Dear Lu,

Don't let mean bullies bother you. Look right at them with eyes fearless. Talk in a voice firm. Look for solutions positive. Find some people friendly to hang with. Being with a group of friends can protect you from bullies nasty.

Your friend,

Brian

Proofreader's Marks

Transpose words, letters:

She said words angry.

See all Proofreader's Marks on page ix.

63 How Do You Use a Predicate Adjective?

After a Form of the Verb *Be*

- Most of the time, **adjectives** come before **nouns**.
  Scott is a **strong kid**. He makes **scary threats**.

- But if your verb is a form of **be**, you can put the adjective after
  the verb. The forms of **be** are **am**, **is**, **are**, **was**, and **were**.
  Scott **is tough**. Other kids **are afraid** of him.

Try It

A. Complete each sentence. Use a predicate adjective from the box.

alone	confident	happier	immature	loyal
rude	stupid	unpleasant	tired	willing

1. Scott's friends were _____ last year.

2. They were _____ to do what Scott said.

3. But Scott was _____ to his friends.

4. "You guys are _____," he said.

5. "I am _____ of listening to Scott," said Marco.

6. "He is so _____."

7. "He is also _____," said Steven.

8. "We are _____ we can do without him," said Juan.

9. His friends are _____ now.

10. Now Scott is _____.

B. Use a predicate adjective to complete each sentence.

11. Some kids at my school are _____ to other people.

12 I am _____ when I pass them in the hall.

13. Last year, one boy was very _____.

14. He said my friends were _____.

15. Now he is _____.

16. We are _____ that he changed.

17. He is _____ that he changed, too!

Write It

C. Answer the questions about bullies. Use predicate adjectives in your answers.

18. Why do some bullies need to be in a group? They _____
_____.

19. How do you feel when a group of kids approaches you? I _____
_____.

20. How do your friends feel about bullies? _____
_____

D. (21–25) Think of a time when you or someone else was bullied. Now write at least five sentences to describe what happened. Use predicate adjectives in your sentences.

_____
_____
_____
_____
_____
_____

64 Why Do You Use a Demonstrative Adjective?

To Point Something Out

- A **demonstrative adjective** signals where something is—either near or far.
- Use **this** and **these** for something near to you.

  This school has a lot of groups.

  I like to do things with **these girls**.
- Use **that** and **those** for something far from you.

  That boy over there never talks to us. He is friendly only with **those kids**.

Demonstrative Adjectives		
	Singular	Plural
Near	this	these
Far	that	those

Try It

A. Complete each sentence. Choose **this**, **that**, **these**, or **those**.

1. That's why we have _____ field day each year.
   this / that

2. _____ event creates harmony.
   This / These

3. We play _____ games with different kids.
   that / these

4. _____ girl over there is a good leader.
   That / This

5. She brings _____ students together.
   that / those

B. Complete the sentences. Use **this**, **that**, **these**, or **those**.

6. At first I didn't want to be on a team with _____ girls.

7. I wanted to be on _____ team with my friends over there.

8. "I hate _____ field day," I thought.

9. Then _____ girl near me asked me to be her partner.

10. Now _____ girls are my friends, too.

Write It

C. Some students at your school want to have a field day. Their idea is to form teams of students who are not already friends. How do you think this would work? Use demonstrative adjectives in your answers.

11. How would you like this idea? I _____

_____.

12. How would this help the students at your school? It would _____

_____.

D. (13–16) Think about an activity or event that might help the students at your school get along. Write at least four sentences about this. Use demonstrative adjectives in your sentences.

_____

_____

_____

_____

_____

_____

Edit It

E. (17–20) Edit the invitation. Fix four mistakes. Use the correct demonstrative adjective.

> ### Come to our School Field Day on Friday!
> This event will be open to everyone. Leave all this old ideas about friends and enemies at home. You will make new friends on these day. Give that games a chance. You will be surprised at how much fun you will have. This games will challenge you. Just try it for a day.

Proofreader's Marks
Change text:
He was first in ~~those~~ that race.
See all Proofreader's Marks on page ix.

65 Use Adjectives to Elaborate

Remember: Use adjectives to add interesting, lively details to your writing. Adjectives help readers see, hear, touch, smell, and taste.

See	Hear	Touch	Smell	Taste
dark	creaky	smooth	sweet	salty
purple	noisy	cold	flowery	bitter
shining	soft	bumpy	moldy	sour

skinny   warm

Ben was a boy who always had a smile.
     ∧   ∧

Try It

A. Add some interesting adjectives to elaborate.

1. Ben greets everyone with a _____ voice.

2. But Anton always gives Ben an _____ glare.

3. Anton yells at people in a _____, _____ voice.

4. Lots of kids think Anton is _____.

5. Everyone except Ben is _____ of him.

B. Add adjectives and rewrite each sentence.

6. One day, Ben brings a bag of snacks to share.

_____

7. The kids give him smiles. _____

_____

8. Anton gives Ben a look and grabs a handful of chips.

_____

9. In a whisper, Ben says, "Just try changing your attitude."

_____

C. Answer the questions about Ben and Anton. Use adjectives to elaborate.

10. How are the two boys different? Anton is _____, but Ben is _____.

11. How can Ben help Anton? Ben _____
_____.

12. What advice would you give Anton? _____
_____

D. (13–16) Now write at least four sentences to tell how kids can influence each other in positive ways.

_____

_____

_____

_____

_____

Edit It

E. (17–20) Improve the journal entry. Change four adjectives to more lively ones.

June 29

How some kids act can be a helpful lesson to others. I think someone with a good attitude can influence mean kids. Sometimes bad kids are just unhappy. They need understanding and someone to show them how to be a good friend.

Proofreader's Marks

Change text: She was ~~happy~~. joyful

See all Proofreader's Marks on page ix.

66 Can You Use an Adjective to Make a Comparison?

Yes, But You Have to Change the Adjective.

- Use a **comparative adjective** to compare two people, places, or things.
  I used to live in a **rough** neighborhood, but this one is **rougher**.
- There are two ways to turn an adjective into a comparative adjective:

1. If the adjective has one syllable, add **-er**. If it has two syllables and ends in a consonant + **y**, change the **y** to **i** before you add **-er**.	**mean** **dark** **happy** **meaner** **darker** **happier**
2. If the adjective has three or more syllables, use **more** before the adjective.	**violent** **miserable** **more violent** **more miserable**

Try It

A. Complete the sentences. Use comparative adjectives.

1. My mother was **worried** when we moved away from Fairview. She is even _____ now here in Bridgeview.

2. The criminals in Fairview were not very **bold**. The ones in Bridgeview are _____.

3. The police are **responsive**, but I wish they were _____.

4. The Fairview police were **slow** to respond, but the Bridgeview police are _____.

5. My neighborhood is **scary** during the day. It is even _____ at night.

6. The community is **agitated**. Every day it becomes _____.

7. I try to be **hopeful**, but I wish I could be _____.

B. Write the comparative form of the adjective in parentheses.

8. The Bridgeview police are _____ than the police in Fairview. (overworked)

9. The crime in Bridgeview is _____ than in Fairview. (dangerous)

10. My family has been _____ than some other families. (lucky)

11. Some of my friends are _____ about crime than I am. (nervous)

12. I wish Bridgeview were _____ than it is. (safe)

Write It

C. (13–15) Now write at least three sentences to tell what might lower the violence in your community. Use comparative adjectives.

_____

_____

_____

_____

Edit It

D. (16–20) Edit the journal entry. Fix five mistakes. Make sure comparative adjectives are in the correct form.

October 27

Last night, we heard loud voices outside. The voices got loud as they came close. My sister was frightened than I was. The voices sounded angry, but I was even angry than they were. I yelled at them to go away. My sister was happy they went away. I was even more happy!

Proofreader's Marks

Change text:
My heart beat ~~fast~~ faster than before.

See all Proofreader's Marks on page ix.

148   © National Geographic Learning, a part of Cengage Learning, Inc.

67 Can an Adjective Compare More Than Two Things?

Yes, But You Have to Use a Different Form.

- A **superlative adjective** compares three or more people, places, or things. To turn an adjective into a superlative adjective:

1. Add **-est** to a one-syllable adjective or to a two-syllable adjective that ends in a consonant + **y**.	Armando's brother was **the strongest** guy in the neighborhood. It was **the rowdiest** neighborhood of all.
2. Use **most** before an adjective of three or more syllables.	He was **the most powerful** kid around.

- Add **the** before the superlative.
- Never use **more** and **-er** together. Never use **most** and **-est** together.

  Armando's brother was the ~~most~~ strongest guy in the neighborhood.

Try It

A. Complete each sentence with the correct adjective.

1. Armando said the _____ things about Edgar.
   meanest / most mean

2. One night he said the _____ thing of all.
   insultingest / most insulting

3. Edgar, Armando, and some other guys got in the _____ fight ever.
   biggest / most big

4. Armando got the _____ of all the fighters.
   more injured / most injured

5. Armando's brother was the _____ of anyone.
   angriest / most angry

6. Luis, the _____ of Edgar's three brothers, had to make a decision.
   youngest / most young

B. Complete each sentence. Use the correct form of the adjective in parentheses.

7. Armando's brother was the _____ kid around. **(tough)**

8. Fighting him was the _____ thing Luis could do. **(dangerous)**

9. It was also the _____ thing. **(scary)**

10. If Luis didn't fight, the others might think he was the _____ kid in the neighborhood. **(cowardly)**

11. But Luis was convinced that fighting was the _____ thing to do. **(pointless)**

12. His heart was the _____ it had ever been. **(heavy)**

13. This was the _____ decision of Luis's life. **(important)**

Write It

C. Answer the questions about Luis. Use comparative and superlative adjectives in your answers.

14. What do you think will happen if Luis fights Armando's brother? If Luis fights Armando's brother, _____ _____.

15. What can Luis do instead of fighting? He can _____ _____.

16. What do you think Luis should do? Luis should _____ _____.

D. (17–20) Do you think a fight ends violence or continues it? Write at least four sentences. Use comparative and superlative adjectives.

_____

_____

_____

_____

_____

Name _____ Date _____

68 Which Adjectives Are Irregular?

Good, Bad, Many, and *Much*

- Some adjectives have special forms.

To Describe 1 Thing	good	bad	many / much
To Compare 2 Things	better	worse	more
To Compare 3 or More Things	best	worst	most

- Use **many** for things you can count. Use **much** for things you can't count.

  How **many** fights are too many?

  How **much** persistence will it take to bring about change?

- How many things are being compared in these sentences?

  Diego wanted his neighborhood to be **better** than it was.

  His neighborhood had the **worst** violence of all the neighborhoods in the city.

Try It

A. Complete each sentence. Use the correct adjective.

1. Diego is _____ at finding solutions.
    good / better

2. He had _____ ideas about stopping violence than his friend did.
    more / most

3. The _____ plan of all was to patrol the neighborhood at night.
    good / best

4. Diego got _____ volunteers to patrol the streets.
    many / most

B. (5–11) Complete each sentence. Use forms of **good**, **bad**, **many**, or **much**.

The amount of crime in the neighborhood was _____ than before.

Then the _____ incident happened since the patrols began. Diego's

_____ friend was killed while patrolling the _____ dangerous

street. But Diego was even _____ convinced that the patrols were a

_____ idea. The neighborhood was still _____ safer than before.

© National Geographic Learning, a part of Cengage Learning, Inc.

151

C. Answer the questions. Use forms of **good**, **bad**, or **many** in your answers.

12. What do you think about Diego's idea? I think _____

_____.

13. What could Diego do to improve the patrols? He could _____

_____.

14. How do you think Diego felt after his friend died? I think he _____

_____.

D. (15–19) Imagine you are Diego. What would you do after your friend died? Write five sentences about this. Use forms of **good**, **bad**, or **many** in your sentences.

_____

_____

_____

_____

_____

Edit It

E. (20–24) Edit the letter. Fix five mistakes. Make sure adjectives are in the correct form.

Dear J.T.,

The violence in my neighborhood is getting worse. Sometimes worst things happen to better people. Yesterday, we heard the worse news. Lupe's brother was killed while he was trying to make his neighborhood a best place. I am most upset now than ever.

Your cousin,

Tanya

Proofreader's Marks
Change text:
The ~~bad~~ thing happened today. (worst)
See all Proofreader's Marks on page ix.

69 When Do You Use an Indefinite Adjective?

When You Can't Be Specific

- If you are not sure of the exact number or amount of something, use an **indefinite adjective**.

  There is **much** violence in our world today.

  A lot of people are affected by it.

  Many teens understand the difference between self-defense and revenge.

  Some kids have done both kinds of fighting.

  Several students fight in self-defense.

- **Many** and **much** are tricky.

  1. Use **many** before a noun, like **fights**, that can be counted.

     Many fights are unnecessary.

  2. Use **much** before a noun, like **pain**, that can't be counted.

     Fighting for revenge causes **much** pain.

Try It

A. Complete each sentence with an indefinite adjective. More than one answer is possible.

1. Martin didn't get into _____ trouble.

2. _____ people thought he was a nice guy.

3. One day, _____ kids surrounded him behind the school.

4. _____ boys started pushing Martin.

5. They yelled _____ threats at him.

6. Martin knew he might have _____ trouble getting away.

7. He didn't believe in _____ fighting, but he had to protect himself.

8. Martin ended up fighting _____ of the boys in self-defense.

B. (9–16) Complete the sentences. Use indefinite adjectives. More than one answer is possible.

After his older brother died in a fight, Cole felt _____ anger. _____ adults told him not to take revenge. But Cole wanted to hurt the people who had caused his family so _____ pain. Cole's younger brothers and _____ of his friends agreed with him. One night they beat up _____ of the teens who had fought Cole's brother. They sent one boy to the hospital. Now _____ of that boy's friends want to get revenge on Cole. _____ people in the neighborhood are worried. They feel there could be _____ of violence. Cole has to think about how he will respond.

Write It

C. Answer the questions about Martin and Cole. Use indefinite adjectives.

17. How are Martin and Cole's situations different? Martin _____. But Cole
   _____.

18. What else could Cole do? He could _____
   _____.

D. (19–20) Do you think there is a difference between fighting in self-defense and fighting for revenge? Write at least two sentences explaining your opinion. Use indefinite adjectives in your sentences.

_____

_____

_____

_____

_____

70 Use Adjectives Correctly

Remember: Use adjectives to describe or compare people, places, or things.

- How do you know which adjective to use?

To Describe 1 Thing	safe	violent	good	many / much
To Compare 2 Things	safer	more violent	better	more
To Compare 3 or More Things	safest	most violent	best	most

Big cities are often **more violent** than small towns. **Many** people think that small towns are **better** places to live. But even the **most violent** city can be **safer**. A city can be a **good** place to live.

Try It

A. **Complete each sentence. Use the correct adjective.**

1. There are _____ reasons for violence.
   many / much

2. Sometimes it happens because the city has so _____ misery.
   many / much

3. _____ teens believe in getting revenge.
   much / some

4. But taking revenge can make the situation _____ than it was.
   worse / worst

5. I think this would be a _____ world if it had no violence.
   gooder / better

B. **(6–10) Complete each sentence with an adjective. More than one answer is possible.**

_____ people accept this city's violence. _____ people lived in cities _____ than this. They say this city is not so _____. The _____ attitude of all is to believe that no violence is acceptable.

C. Answer the questions about violence. Use adjectives in the correct form.

11. How does living in a violent community affect people? People _____

_____.

12. Do you think there are any good reasons for violence? I think _____

_____.

D. (13–16) How do you think the world would be different if people didn't accept violence? Write at least four sentences. Use adjectives in the correct form.

_____

_____

_____

_____

_____

_____

Edit It

E. (17–20) Edit the journal entry. Fix four mistakes. Make sure adjectives are in the correct form.

June 10

The world is getting scarier every day. But I don't think it has to be such a worse place. If much people refused to accept violence, I would be happiest. The best attitude of all is to believe that any violence is not acceptable. Much people think we can reduce violence. I agree!

Proofreader's Marks

Delete:

There is a lot of much violence.

Change text: better

We will feel best than before.

See all Proofreader's Marks on page ix.

71 Why Do You Need Adverbs?

To Tell *How*, *When*, or *Where*

- Use an **adverb** to describe a verb. Adverbs often end in **-ly**.

  My friends and I like other people to behave **politely** at the movies. (how)

  We don't like people sitting **close** to us. (where)

  If people bump me, I like them to apologize **promptly**. (when)

- Use an **adverb** to make another adverb or an adjective stronger.

  Some people talk **very** loudly during the movie.
  adverb

  I think that is **really** rude.
  adjective

- Adverbs add details and bring life to your writing.

  My brother Carlos was **quite** upset about something that happened **yesterday**. He **excitedly** told me about it when he got home.

Try It

A. **Complete the sentences. Use adverbs to add details.**

1. Carlos was at a _____ crowded basketball game.

2. He heard someone yelling _____.

3. Carlos looked _____.

4. A man was being _____ rude.

5. He yelled _____ insulting words.

B. **(6–11) Use adverbs to complete the story.**

The man waved his arms _____ and refused to sit

_____. The people nearby watched _____. Someone

_____ asked the man to be quiet. The man refused. A security guard

_____ removed the man. Everyone applauded _____.

C. Answer the questions about Carlos's story. Use adverbs in your answers.

12. How do you think Carlos felt when the man was rude? He _____

_____.

13. What if the man were still there? What might happen? The other people _____

_____

14. How do you feel about people who insult others? _____

_____

15. What can you do if someone insults you? _____

_____

D. (16–19) Think of a time you saw someone who was rude. Write at least four sentences to tell what happened. Use adverbs.

_____

_____

_____

_____

_____

Edit It

E. (20–25) Improve the letter. Use six adverbs to make the sentences more interesting.

Dear Jo,

What an upsetting time that was at the movies yesterday!
Thanks for telling that guy in the movie to sit. He was talking
and it was making me mad. Some people can be insensitive. They
should think about how behaving disturbs others.

Your friend,

Todd

Proofreader's Marks

Add text:
                very
He was ˄ rude.

See all Proofreader's Marks on page ix.

72 What Happens When You Add *Not* to a Sentence?

You Make the Sentence Negative.

- The word **not** is an adverb. Add it to a sentence to make it negative. If the verb is an **action verb**, change the sentence like this:
  I **have** a friend named Ed. I **do not have** a friend named Ed.

- If the verb is a form of **be**, just place **not** after the verb:
  He **is** very smart. He **is not** very smart.

- When you shorten a verb plus **not**, replace the **o** in **not** with an apostrophe (').

  1. Ed **does not** have many friends.

  Ed **doesn't** have many friends.

  2. He **is not** easy to like.

  He **isn't** easy to like.

Try It

A. Make these sentences negative.

1. Sometimes Ed says the right thing. _____

_____

2. Ed is always polite. _____

_____

3. Most people enjoy his rudeness. _____

_____

4. I know whom to invite to my party. _____

_____

5. I want to invite Ed. _____

_____

6. Most of my friends like him. _____

_____

B. Use the verbs in parentheses to make each sentence negative.

7. Some people _____ it is cool to be polite. **(think)**

8. They _____ about other people's feelings. **(care)**

9. But others _____ to be around rude people. **(like)**

10. They _____ to be insulted. **(want)**

11. Most people _____ rude behavior. **(admire)**

12. They _____ confronting rude people. **(enjoy)**

13. But rude people _____ the rules. **(obey)**

14. We _____ the problem. **(ignore)**

Write It

C. What would happen if one of your friends said insulting things about your other friends? Use **not** to make some of your sentences negative.

15. How would it make you feel? I _____
_____.

16. What could you do about it? If my friend said something insulting, _____
_____.

D. (17–20) Think about someone you know who is rude. Write at least four sentences telling how other people react to this person's rudeness. Use *not* to make some of your sentences negative.

_____

_____

_____

_____

_____

73 How Do You Make a Sentence Negative?

Use One, and Only One, Negative Word.

- These words are negative words: **no**, **nobody**, **nothing**, **no one**, **not**, **never**, **nowhere**, and **none**.

- Use only one negative word in a sentence.

Incorrect:	I never met no one like Sergey before.
Correct:	I never met anyone like Sergey before.
Incorrect:	He doesn't care about nobody else's feelings.
Correct:	He doesn't care about anybody else's feelings.
Incorrect:	He doesn't have no friends.
Correct:	He doesn't have any friends.
Correct:	He has no friends.

Try It

A. Fix each sentence to use only one negative word.

1–2. Sergey didn't have nothing nice to say about nobody.

3. He said I didn't have no nice clothes.

4. No one had never been so insulting.

5. I was not never more offended.

6. I didn't want nothing to do with Sergey.

7. I would never say nothing like that.

8. There isn't nobody who has a right to judge another.

Proofreader's Marks

Delete:

He was ~~not~~ never rude.

Change text:
was
I ~~wasn't~~ never rude.

See all Proofreader's Marks on page ix.

B. Make each sentence negative. Use only one negative word. There is more than one possible answer.

9. I wanted to say something to Sergey. _____

10. "I liked what you said about my clothes," I said. _____
_____

11. "I have something else to wear." _____

12. "Something you said made me happy." _____

13. Sergey said, "I'll say something like that again." _____
_____

Write It

C. Imagine one of your friends says something insulting to another friend of yours. Write about how you deal with it. Make some of your sentences negative.

14. How do you feel when you hear your friend insulted? I _____
_____.

15. What do you say to the friend who was insulted? You _____
_____.

16. What do you tell the friend who was rude? It _____
_____.

D. (17–20) Think about a time someone said something insulting to you. Write at least four sentences telling what happened. Make some of your sentences negative.

_____
_____
_____
_____
_____

74 Can You Use an Adverb to Make a Comparison?

Yes, But You Need to Change the Adverb.

- Adverbs have different forms. Use the form that fits your purpose.

To Describe 1 Action	soon	loudly	well	badly
To Compare 2 Actions	sooner	more loudly	better	worse
To Compare 3 or More Actions	soonest	most loudly	best	worst

- Think about how many things are being compared in these sentences:
  Some people speak **more carefully** than others.
  People who are kind may speak the **most carefully** of all.

Try It

A. Complete each sentence with the correct adverb.

1. Some people try _____ than others to be kind.
   harder / hardest

2. Telling the truth works _____ than telling lies.
   best / better

3. People can learn to speak _____.
   sensitively / most sensitively

4. Kind, cautious people may express themselves _____ of all.
   well / best

B. Complete each sentence. Use a comparison form of the adverb in parentheses.

5. Maya acted _____ of all her friends. **(honestly)**

6. She spoke _____ than her friend Zoe did. **(boldly)**

7. Zoe thought _____ than Maya did about others' feelings. **(hard)**

8. Sometimes the entire truth hurts _____ than kind words. **(badly)**

9. Maya is behaving _____ now than she did before. **(well)**

C. Answer the questions about honesty. Use comparison adverbs.

10. Why do you think some people find it hard to be completely honest? They _____

_____.

11. Why is being sensitive and honest more challenging than just being honest? It is _____

_____.

D. (12–15) Do you think it is good to be completely honest even if it hurts someone? Write at least four sentences explaining your opinion. Use comparison adverbs in your sentences.

_____

_____

_____

_____

_____

E. (16–20) Edit the journal entry below. Fix five mistakes. Make sure adverbs are in the correct form.

May 15

I am worried that I treated Ayla badly. She wanted my opinion of her dancing. I told her she danced gracefully than Renate, but that isn't what I really think. Will it work well to tell her the truth or not to hurt her feelings? A person who speaks honestly might behave worser than one who keeps silent. Of all my friends, she's the one I want to speak to the more honestly. I should act best than I did before.

Proofreader's Marks

Change text:
I spoke most harshly than before. (more)

Add text:
You sang the beautifully of all. (most)

See all Proofreader's Marks on page ix.

75 Use Adverbs Correctly

Remember: You can use adverbs to describe and compare actions.
An adverb can also make another adverb or adjective stronger.

Describe	Compare	Make Stronger
I did not speak **kindly** to my grandmother.	I know I should behave **better** around her.	I acted **very** badly.
My parents taught me to treat her **respectfully**.	I should treat her **more sensitively**.	My grandmother is **really** upset.

Try It

A. Use an adverb from the box to complete each sentence.

more wisely	nervously	quietly	really	softly

1. My grandmother entered the room _____.

2. I looked _____ at her.

3. I was _____ embarrassed.

4. She spoke _____ to me.

5. "You should speak _____ than you did," she said.

B. (6–10) Complete each sentence with an adverb. More than one answer is possible.

My grandmother said I should choose my words _____ in the future. I understood her _____. If I speak too _____, it can be _____ harmful. From now on I will treat people the _____ that I can.

Write It

C. Answer the questions about how to speak without hurting people's feelings. Use adverbs.

11. Why is it a good idea to think before you speak? If you don't _____

_____.

12. How do you think people should speak to each other? I think _____

_____.

D. (13–16) Think about a time your words hurt someone. Write at least four sentences to tell what happened. Use adverbs.

_____

_____

_____

_____

_____

Edit It

E. (17–20) Edit the letter. Fix four mistakes.

Dear Mike,

   I want to quickly apologize for my behavior yesterday. I am much sorry that I spoke so rude to you. I know I hurt your feelings worse. I promise I will treat you best from now on. I made a mistake and I am sorry. I hope you can forgive me.

Sincerely,

Sam

Proofreader's Marks

Change text:

She treated me ~~bad.~~ badly

See all Proofreader's Marks on page ix.

✔ Capitalize the Proper Nouns and Adjectives

- **Proper nouns** are capitalized because they name specific people, places, and things. Common nouns, which are general, are not capitalized.

Common Noun	Proper Noun
cat	Mugsy
month	September

- **Proper adjectives**, which come from proper nouns, are also capitalized.

Proper Noun	Proper Adjective
France	French
Australia	Australian

Try It

A. Use proofreader's marks to correct the capitalization error in each sentence.

1. Shondra wants to train her dog, daisy.

2. Daisy is part german shepherd and part Irish terrier.

3. Shondra took Daisy to a Dog training school.

4. Daisy will start taking classes in june.

5. There are two Poodles, three terriers, and a beagle in Daisy's class.

6. Next week, Shondra will take Daisy to a dog show in florida.

B. (7–8) Write at least two sentences about general and specific places you would like to visit. Tell why you want to visit these places. Capitalize correctly.

_____

_____

_____

Proofreader's Marks

Capitalize:

She has a ₌french poodle.

Do not capitalize:

My favorite Month is May.

See all Proofreader's Marks on page ix.

✔ Punctuate Introductory Words and Clauses Correctly

- Place a comma after introductory words such as **yes, no, first,** and **next,** and adverbs such as **happily** and **unfortunately.**

  First, we need to get dog treats to give as a reward.
  Fortunately, we already have some dog treats.

- Place a comma after long or introductory clauses.
  When you are ready, we will get started.
  After you give the dog a treat, pat and praise it, too.

Try It

A. (9–15) Edit the description of how to train a dog to get things for you. Fix seven punctuation mistakes.

There are several ways to train a dog to get things for you. If you really want to train your dog well the best way is to reward it with treats. Before, you get started gather the materials you will need. First you will need a household object, such as a glove, that your dog can use for practice. Then you will need dog treats, to give as reward. When you have all the materials you are ready to begin training your dog.

Proofreader's Marks

Add a comma:

Yesˏ I trained your dog.

Delete:

I taught your dog ͯto retrieve things.

✓ Check Your Spelling

Follow these rules for spelling words with **ie** and **ei**:

1. Use **i** before **e** except after **c**.
   Examples: bel**ie**f, p**ie**ce

2. For a long **a** or **ar** sound, use **ei**.
   Examples: fr**ei**ght, th**ei**r

3. For a long **e** sound after **c**, use **ei**.
   Examples: c**ei**ling, dec**ei**ve

Memorize these exceptions to the rules: **achieve, either, neither, science, seize.**

Try It

Proofreader's Marks

Change text:
Her ~~neice~~ niece adopted a
dog. ∧

A. Choose the correctly spelled word to complete each sentence.

16. Our _____ has two cats and a dog.
    neighbor / nieghbor

17. Their dog Wrigley loves to _____ things and bring them back to you.
    retreive / retrieve

18. Each time Wrigley _____ success, they give him a treat.
    achieves / acheives

19. The two cats, Stella and Sam, also _____ treats.
    receive / recieve

B. (20–23) Edit the cat adoption application. Fix four spelling mistakes.

Do you have any other pets? How long have you had the pet? _____Yes, we have one cat._____

We have had him for ieght years.

Why do you want to adopt a cat? _____We want our cat Langston to have a freind at home._____

We love animals, but my dad is allergic to dogs. Niether one of us is allergic to cats.

Why do you think you would be a good pet owner? _____I beleive that we are good pet owners_____
because we take good care of Langston. He is in good health and seems to be very happy.

✓ Use Adjectives and Adverbs Correctly

- Usually the adjective comes before the noun it describes. But a predicate adjective appears in the predicate and still describes the noun in the subject.

  Mugsy is a **fluffy** cat.

  subject   adjective noun

  She is **playful**, too.

  subject   adjective

- An adjective is never plural, even if the noun it describes is plural.

  Olivia took care of the **older** cats at the shelter. Ray trained the **new** dogs.

  adjective noun   adjective noun

- If you want to describe a verb, use an adverb, not an adjective.

  Incorrect: The cat ate **slow**.

  verb adjective

  Correct: The cat ate **slowly**.

  verb adverb

- Never use an adverb after a linking verb.

  Incorrect: Ray is **patiently** with the dogs.

  linking adverb
  verb

  Correct: Ray is **patient** with the dogs.

  linking adjective
  verb

Try It

A. Complete each sentence with an adjective or adverb from the box.

amazingly	delicious	large	old	quickly

24. Ray taught one of the _____ dogs, Pippin, how to retrieve things.

25. Pippin learned _____ because it seemed like a game.

26. Ray used an _____ glove for Pippin to practice with.

27. _____, Pippin retrieved the glove on his first try.

28. Each time Pippin learned a new step, Ray gave him a _____ treat.

B. Use the adjective or adverb to write a sentence about animals.

29. (slow) _____

30. (slowly) _____

76 What's a Simple Sentence?

A Sentence with One Subject and One Predicate

- A sentence expresses a complete thought. It has a **subject** and a **predicate**. The most important word in the predicate is the **verb**.
  Jenny **is** in the political action club.

- Often, the subject is a **noun** that names a specific person, place, or thing.
  Mrs. Adams **advises** the club.
  All the **students** **enjoy** politics.

- Sometimes, the subject is a **pronoun** that stands for a noun.
  They often **volunteer** during elections.

Try It

A. Rewrite each sentence. Replace the subject with a subject pronoun. Use **he**, **she**, **it**, or **they**.

1. Marcus is in the political action club. _____

2. The club members discuss the local election. _____

3. Mr. Wilson is running for the state senate. _____

4. That job is important. _____

5. Kichi wants to volunteer on the campaign. _____

B. Add a subject pronoun to complete each sentence.

6. Kichi and Marcus both volunteer. _____ make phone calls for the campaign.

7. Marcus is old enough to drive. _____ delivers campaign leaflets.

8. An editorial appears in the local paper. _____ is about Kichi and Marcus.

9. The writer thinks the voting age should be lowered. _____ thinks sixteen-year-olds should be allowed to vote.

C. Marcus and Kichi are volunteering on a campaign, but they are not allowed to vote. What do you think about that? Write four simple sentences.

10. _____

11. _____

12. _____

13. _____

D. (14–15) Now write at least two simple sentences about an election in your area.

_____

_____

_____

Edit It

E. (16–20) Edit the conversation. Add five subjects.

Marcus: It's not fair. Seventeen-year-olds are old enough to work but not to vote.

Kichi: But Marcus, not all teens understand the issues. don't know who they want to vote for.

Marcus: I know who I want to vote for. Am ready for the responsibility.

Kichi: Marcus, can't vote until you're 18. It's the law.

Marcus: will be 18 soon. Then will vote in every election!

Proofreader's Marks
Add text:
Yesterday, voted.
Do not capitalize:
I Volunteer my time.
See all Proofreader's Marks on page ix.

77 When Do You Use an Indefinite Pronoun?

When You Can't Be Specific

- When you are not talking about a specific person or thing, you can use an **indefinite pronoun**.

  Everyone thinks it is easy to be a teenager. **Nothing** is ever easy!

- Some indefinite pronouns are always singular, so they need a **singular verb** that ends in **-s**.

  No one understand**s** us kids. **Someone** tell**s** us what to do all the time!

Singular Indefinite Pronouns			
another	each	everything	nothing
anybody	either	neither	somebody
anyone	everybody	nobody	someone
anything	everyone	no one	something

Try It

A. Complete each sentence. Write the correct verb.

1. Homework or chores? Neither _____ me happy.
   make / makes

2. Each _____ to be done before I can have free time.
   need / needs

3. Nobody _____ how hard it is to be a teen.
   understand / understands

4. "You can't use the car. I need it," someone always _____.
   exclaim / exclaims

5. Anything _____ easier than being a teen!
   seem / seems

6. No one _____ what it's like to be a teen.
   remember / remembers

7. Something _____ when a teen grows up, I guess.
   happen / happens

B. Use words from each column to write five sentences about being a teenager. You can use words more than once.

Everybody	believes	it's fun to be a teen.
Everyone	wants	to grow up.
Nobody	prevents	the teenage years are the best.
No one	frustrates	teens from having fun.
Everything	thinks	teens.

8. _____

9. _____

10. _____

11. _____

12. _____

Write It

C. Complete the sentences. Tell about teen life. Use correct verbs to match the indefinite pronouns.

13. Each of the students _____.

14. Everybody in my class _____.

15. No one in my family _____.

16. Nothing about my life _____.

D. (17–20) How do you feel about being a teenager? Write at least four sentences. Use indefinite pronouns.

_____

_____

_____

_____

_____

78 Which Indefinite Pronouns Are Plural?

Both, Few, Many, and Several

- Use an **indefinite pronoun** when you are not talking about a specific person or thing.

  Both of my parents help me.

  Many of my teachers do, too.

- Some **indefinite pronouns** are always plural, so they need a **plural verb**.

  Several give me references for jobs.

  A **few** share good books with me.

Plural Indefinite Pronouns	
both	many
few	several

Try It

A. Write the correct form of the verb to complete each sentence.

1. Both of my parents _____ me do to my best.
   encourage / encourages

2. Many of their suggestions _____ me for the adult world.
   prepare / prepares

3. Some of their suggestions _____ me to valuable experiences.
   lead / leads

4. Several _____ me to books and resources.
   direct / directs

5. A few _____ me about what not to do when I become an adult.
   teach / teaches

B. (6–10) Write plural indefinite pronouns to complete the paragraph.

_____ of the adults I know are positive role models for

teens. _____ of my teachers organized a field trip this summer.

A _____ of us students helped build houses. _____ of these

experiences contained valuable lessons. _____ prepared me for the

adult world.

C. Use these indefinite pronouns to write sentences. Tell how people have prepared you for the adult world. Use the correct form of the verb.

11. Both _____.

12. Many _____.

13. A few _____.

14. Several _____.

D. (15–18) Now write at least four sentences that tell more about people who have helped you prepare for the adult world. Use plural indefinite pronouns.

_____

_____

_____

_____

Edit It

E. (19–25) Edit the journal entry. Fix seven verb mistakes.

April 3

It is Mother-Daughter Day. Some of the
mothers work at a nursing home. Many
daughters visits there. Several helps with the
patients. Many of the patients is glad to see
me. A few asks what I study at school. Two
patients are playing cards. Both wants me
to play with them. Several patients shares
stories about their lives. Many of them wants
me to come back next year.

Proofreader's Marks

Change text:

A few likes to sing.

See all Proofreader's Marks on page ix.

79 Which Indefinite Pronouns Are Tricky?

The Ones That Can Be Singular or Plural

- The **indefinite pronouns** in the chart can be either singular or plural.

- The prepositional phrase after the pronoun shows whether the sentence talks about one thing or more than one thing. Use the correct **verb**.

  Singular: **Most** of my **family volunteers** at the food kitchen.

  Plural: **Most** of my **friends volunteer** there, too.

  Singular: **Some** of the **work is** creative.
  Plural: **Some** of the **jobs are** fun.

Singular or Plural Indefinite Pronouns	
all	none
any	some
most	

Try It

A. Write the correct form of the verb to complete each sentence.

1. Most of my friends _____ volunteer work.
    do / does

2. In that way, some of them _____ about life's realities.
    learn / learns

3. Some of the work _____ hard, physical labor.
    is / are

4. For example, most of the park work _____ digging and planting.
    require / requires

5. At the animal shelter, none of my chores _____ too difficult.
    is / are

6. All of my duties _____ taking care of the animals.
    involve / involves

7. Some of the hospital volunteers _____ to be nurses some day.
    wants / want

B. Choose words from each column to build four sentences. You can use words more than once.

All of the group	work	in inner city programs.
Some of the teenagers	works	about the environment.
Most of my friends	care	about social issues.
Some of the volunteer staff	cares	at the soup kitchen.

8. _____.

9. _____.

10. _____.

11. _____.

Write It

C. Complete the sentences about social issues. Use the correct form of the verb.

12. Some of the important social issues _____.

13. To help with conserving energy, most of my friends _____ _____.

14. Because it is important to have a clean environment, none of my family _____ _____.

15. Some of the students in my class _____.

D. (16–20) What social issue is important to you? How can you help? Write at least five sentences. Use indefinite pronouns.

_____

_____

_____

_____

_____

80 Use Indefinite Pronouns

Remember: Use an indefinite pronoun when you are not talking about a specific person, place, or thing.

The verb you use depends on the indefinite pronoun.

- Some indefinite pronouns are always singular.
  Everybody votes in the election.
  Someone wins, and **someone loses**.

- Some indefinite pronouns are always plural.
  Both of my best friends **run** in our student council election.
  Several of the students **vote** for them.

- Some indefinite pronouns can be singular or plural.
  The prepositional phrase tells which verb to use.
  All of the voting **is** over.
  All of the ballots **are** in the ballot box.

Try It

A. Write an indefinite pronoun to complete each sentence. More than one answer is possible.

1. _____ in our school can vote in the student election.

2. _____ of the students do vote, too.

3. That's because _____ wants a say in the student government.

B. Write the correct form of the verb in parentheses.

4. At my school, everyone in student government _____ hard. **(work)**

5. That's because most of the issues _____ all the students. **(affect)**

6. All of the student government officers _____ good leaders. **(be)**

7. Each _____ the majority of students in the school. **(represent)**

Write It

C. Answer the questions about your school's student government. Use indefinite pronouns.

8. Who votes in student elections? _____

9. What do the student representatives do? _____

10. How does the student body feel about their student government? _____

_____

D. (11–13) What is an important issue at your school? Write at least three sentences. Use indefinite pronouns.

_____

_____

_____

_____

Edit It

E. (14–20) Edit this editorial about the voting age. Fix the seven verb mistakes.

Should Teens Get to Vote?

Everyone has the right to vote. Well, not actually everyone, because you has to be 18 to vote. Something about that do not seem fair to this writer. Many of the younger teens drives, and some of us works, too. Everybody have a political opinion, but several of us is not old enough to vote. Nothing are as important as the right to vote. This writer believes that the voting age should be lowered to 16.

Proofreader's Marks

Change text:

Some of the research shows~~shows~~ ^show facts about teens and voting.

See all Proofreader's Marks on page ix.

81 Where Do You Put the Subject?

Usually Before the Predicate

- Every sentence has a **subject** and a **predicate**. The verb is the most important part of the predicate.

   The **teens walked**.   The **curfew began**.   The **people left**.
     subject predicate   subject predicate   subject predicate

- English sentences usually follow this pattern: **subject → verb → object**.

   The **city had** a **curfew**.   **Jeremy left** the **city**.
     subject verb   object   subject verb   object

Try It

A. **Put the words in the right order. Write the new sentence. Punctuate your sentences correctly.**

1. a curfew / has / our town _____

2. the curfew / most of the students / don't like _____
_____

3. the student government / some plans / developed _____
_____

4. give / good students some benefits / the plans _____
_____

5. alternatives to the curfew / present / most of the plans _____
_____

6. gives / one of the plans / passes to students with good grades. _____
_____

7. good students to stay out late / the passes / allow _____
_____

8. earn / free passes for students / good grades _____
_____

B. Choose words from each column to build four sentences about curfews. You can use words more than once.

Many cities	present	alternatives to curfews.
Curfews	obey	teens from staying out late.
Most teenagers	keep	the rules.
Some parents	have	that teenage years are the best.
		curfews.

9. _____

10. _____

11. _____

12. _____

Write It

C. Complete the sentences about curfews. Use subject-verb or subject-verb-object order.

13. Curfews _____.

14. Most teens _____.

15. Teens who cause trouble _____.

16. Cities _____.

D. (17–20) Write at least four sentences about keeping city streets safe at night. Use subject-verb or subject-verb-object order.

_____

_____

_____

_____

_____

82 Where Do You Put the Negative Word?

In the Subject, Object, or near the Verb

- A negative sentence has one **negative word**.

- The negative word comes between a helping verb and a main verb. The word order of the sentence does not change.

  subject
  A lot of teens do **not** communicate with their parents.
  helping   verb   object
  verb

  subject
  Some parents will **never** know the truth.
  helping   verb   object
  verb

Negative Words	
never	no one
no	nobody
not	nothing
none	nowhere

- The negative word can be the subject or the object in a sentence. The word order does not change.

  Nobody wants trouble.   Trouble helps **nobody**.
  subject   verb   object   subject   verb   object

Try It

A. Make the sentences negative. Add a negative word to each sentence.

1. City streets are _____ always safe.

2. _____ should walk down unlighted streets.

3. Teens should _____ wander into dangerous neighborhoods.

4. Safety is _____ all about curfews.

B. Rewrite each sentence to make it a negative sentence.

5. Teens are safe at night. _____

6. Some teens tell their parents everything. _____

7. Some situations are safe. _____

C. What do you think teenagers can do to be safe? Write three rules using a negative word in each.

8. _____

9. _____

10. _____

D. (11–15) Write at least five sentences that tell how parents and teens can work together to keep teens safe. Use at least five negative words.

_____
_____
_____
_____
_____

Edit It

E. (16–20) Edit the list of statements about teen safety. Add or change words to make each statement a negative sentence.

Safety Rules

Teens should never drive alone at night.
Cars with too many passengers are safe either.
Every street is free from danger.
Busy highways are safe.
People should walk to a parked car alone at night.
Do use cell phones while driving.

Proofreader's Marks

Add text:
never
We stay out late.

Change text:
No
All rules were broken.

See all Proofreader's Marks on page ix.

© National Geographic Learning, a part of Cengage Learning, Inc.

83 Does the Subject Always Come First?

Not Always

> You can begin a sentence with **there is** or **there are**.
> Then the subject comes after the verb.
>
> - Use **there is** for singular subjects.
>   **There is** a good **reason** for my son's curfew.
>   verb   subject
>
> - Use **there are** for plural subjects.
>   **There are** good **reasons** for my son's curfew.
>   verb   subject

Try It

A. Write **there is** or **there are** to complete each sentence about teen responsibility. Then underline the subject of the sentence.

1. _____ consequences to my actions.
   There is / There are

2. Sometimes _____ an uncompleted chore.
   there is / there are

3. Then _____ a punishment.
   there is / there are

4. Other times, _____ broken curfews.
   there is / there are

5. After that, _____ a new curfew.
   there is / there are

B. (6–10) Write **is** or **are** to complete the paragraph about responsibility. Then underline the subjects.

In my house, there _____ rewards for being responsible. There _____ an allowance for finishing chores. There _____ extra bonuses, such as borrowing the car. Then, there _____ the best incentive of all. If I earn my parents' trust, there _____ a later curfew on weekend nights.

185

C. Write sentences about responsibilities that might help you gain more freedom. Begin each sentence with **There is** or **There are**. Use the subjects in parentheses.

11. (times) _____

12. (homework) _____

13. (behavior) _____

14. (chores) _____

D. (15–18) Do you think parents should impose curfews on their teens? How could teens convince their parents not to impose the curfews? Write at least four sentences that begin with **There is** or **There are**.

_____

_____

_____

_____

_____

E. (19–25) Edit the newspaper article about curfews at a local mall. Correct seven mistakes.

Curfew at the Mall

There is a new idea at the mall. Due to recent vandalism, the management are imposing a curfew. There is new rules. First, there are no curfew for anyone before 9:00 p.m. Second, there are a 9:00 p.m. curfew for everyone under 20. There is no unsupervised teens after 9:00 p.m. There is things teens can do to try to change this new rule. They can behave more responsibly. If there are no vandalism, a curfew won't be necessary.

Proofreader's Marks

Change text:
There is new rules. → are

See all Proofreader's Marks on page ix.

84 When Does the Word Order Change?

In Questions and Exclamations

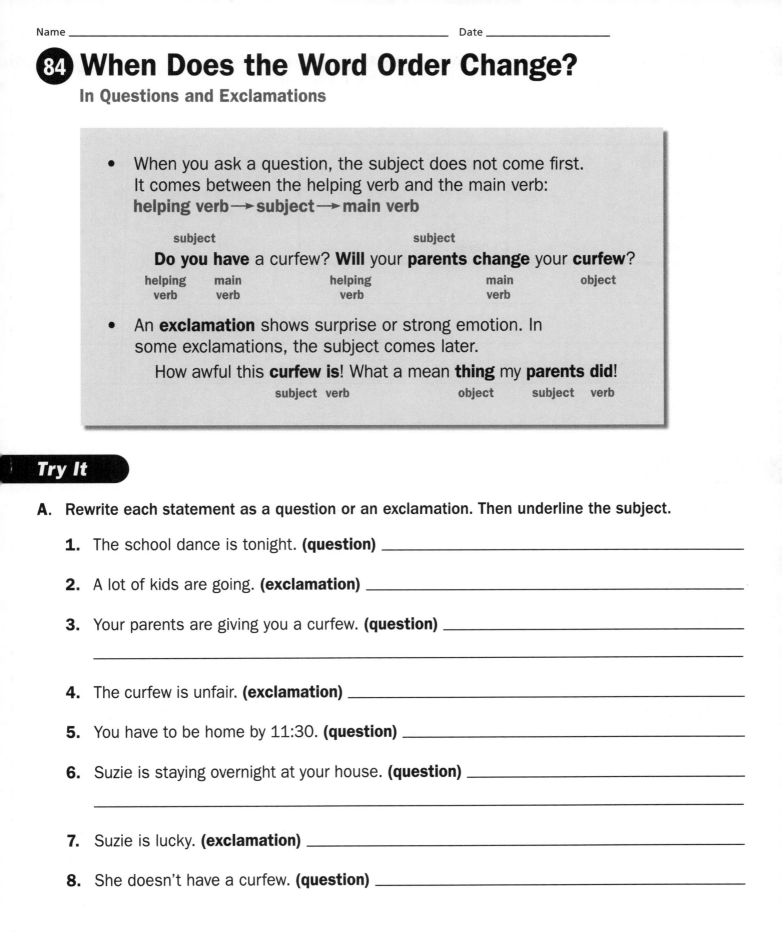

- When you ask a question, the subject does not come first. It comes between the helping verb and the main verb:

  helping verb → subject → main verb

  | subject | | subject |

  Do you have a curfew? **Will** your **parents change** your **curfew**?

  helping   main   helping   main   object
  verb   verb   verb   verb

- An **exclamation** shows surprise or strong emotion. In some exclamations, the subject comes later.

  How awful this **curfew is**! What a mean **thing** my **parents did**!

  subject verb   object   subject   verb

Try It

A. Rewrite each statement as a question or an exclamation. Then underline the subject.

1. The school dance is tonight. **(question)** _____

2. A lot of kids are going. **(exclamation)** _____

3. Your parents are giving you a curfew. **(question)** _____

   _____

4. The curfew is unfair. **(exclamation)** _____

5. You have to be home by 11:30. **(question)** _____

6. Suzie is staying overnight at your house. **(question)** _____

   _____

7. Suzie is lucky. **(exclamation)** _____

8. She doesn't have a curfew. **(question)** _____

B. Use words from each column to create two questions and two exclamations about curfews and parents. You can use words more than once.

Subjects	Verbs
your mom	is giving
Ben	has
the dance	is
Sara	hates

9. _____

10. _____

11. _____

12. _____

Write It

C. Write questions or exclamations to complete the conversation between two teens.

13. Are you _____ Yes, I am going to the movies.

14. Do you _____ No, I don't have a curfew tonight!

15. Wow! How _____

16. _____

D. (17–20) What do your friends and you think about your parents' rules regarding curfews? Write a conversation. Use at least two questions and two exclamations.

_____

_____

_____

_____

_____

85 Vary Your Sentences

Remember: You can make your writing more interesting when you include a question or an exclamation, or use **there is** or **there are**.

To vary your sentences, you can:

- Use **there is** or **there are**.

  Laura and her parents disagree. ∧ There are Ways to compromise ~~are needed.~~

- Include a question or an exclamation in a group of statements.

  Laura wants a later curfew. ~~She will change her behavior.~~ Will she change her behavior? Laura's parents appreciate her efforts. ~~They are pleased.~~ ∧ How pleased they are! Now, both Laura and her parents get what they want.

Try It

A. Write each sentence in another way. More than one answer is possible.

1. Reasons for Mom's anger exist. _____

2. I can change that. _____

3. I will try harder. _____

4. Good behavior makes a big difference. _____

5. Now room for a compromise with Mom exists. _____

   _____

B. Write words to complete each sentence.

6. _____ you try to compromise with your mom?

7. _____ a way to come to an agreement.

8. _____ getting good grades makes!

9. _____ you think your mom will let you stay out later now?

C. Your friend has reached an agreement with her parents. She will change her behavior, and her parents will give her a later curfew. Complete the statement, the exclamation, and the question to tell about the agreement.

10. There are _____

_____.

11. How _____

_____!

12. Will _____

_____?

D. (13–15) What agreements have you made with your parents? Write a statement, a question, and an exclamation that tell about your agreements.

_____

_____

_____

E. (16–20) Edit this conversation between two teens. Rewrite five of the sentences to make the conversation more interesting.

Roger: You know about the curfew my parents gave me.

Rachel: That curfew is awful.

Roger: Well, I've made a compromise with them.

Rachel: You can go out and have more fun now.

Roger: I must do some things first. I have to bring up my grades and do my chores. Then I can stay out until midnight on weekends.

Rachel: That is a great compromise.

Proofreader's Marks
Change text:
How great it will be!
It will be great.
See all Proofreader's Marks on page ix.

86 How Are Phrases and Clauses Different?

A Clause Has a Subject and a Predicate.

- A **phrase** is a group of words that function together. One sentence often has several phrases.

    A motivated **girl** / from my biology class / **volunteers** / weekends / at the hospital.
    noun phrase   adjective phrase   verb   adverb   adverb phrase

    This sentence is complete because it has a **subject** and a **verb**.
    A phrase never has both, so it does not express a complete thought.

- A **clause** contains a **subject** and a **verb**. An independent clause can stand alone as a sentence.

    The **girl learned** about different hospital careers.

- **Clauses** that begin with words like **when, because,** and **if** cannot stand alone.

    When **she worked** in the lab.

Try It

A. Underline the phrase in each sentence about Christina. Then rewrite the sentence using a different phrase.

1. Christina attended a local college. _____

2. She learned about biology. _____

3. After four years, Christina graduated from college. _____

    _____

4. She went to graduate school. _____

5. Now, Christina works as a nurse practitioner. _____

    _____

6. After all that preparation, she loves working. _____

    _____

B. Write the sentences again. Add the phrases in parentheses.

7. Nick wants to work. **(in the computer industry)** _____

_____

8. The guidance counselor helps Nick. **(at his high school)** _____

_____

9. Nicks learns information. **(about careers in computer science)** _____

_____

10. Most have gone to college. **(of the computer engineers)** _____

_____

11. The engineers get good jobs. **(After college,)** _____

_____

Write It

C. What do you want to do after high school? Complete the sentences. Use at least one additional phrase in each sentence.

12. After high school, I want _____.

13. To do that, I will need _____.

14. People in that career _____.

15. So far, my work experience includes _____.

D. (16–18) What kind of work interests you? Write at least three questions you would like to ask of someone who does that kind of work. Use at least one phrase in each question.

_____

_____

_____

_____

_____

87 What's a Compound Sentence?

Two Independent Clauses Joined by *And*, *But*, or *Or*

The words **and**, **but**, and **or** are conjunctions. They join the two independent clauses in a **compound sentence**. A comma (**,**) comes before the conjunction.

- Use **and** to join similar ideas.

  Julia needs to rent an apartment.
  It must be near her job.

  Julia needs to rent an apartment, and it must be near her job.

- Use **but** to join different ideas.

  Julia finds a nice apartment.
  It is too expensive.

  Julia finds a nice apartment, but it is too expensive.

- Use **or** to show a choice.

  Julia can look for a roommate.
  She can find a cheaper apartment.

  Julia can look for a roommate, or she can find a cheaper apartment.

Try It

A. Use and, but, or or to rewrite each pair of sentences as one compound sentence.

1. Julio lives at home. He just got a job in a different state.

2. He needs to move. He wants a nice apartment.

3. A nice apartment will be expensive. Julio needs to rent one.

4. Julio can look in the newspaper. He can call a real estate agent.

B. These compound sentences are missing and, but, or or. Fix the mistakes.

5. Julio sees one apartment it is perfect.

6. He wants to rent the apartment it is too expensive.

7. Julio can rent this apartment he can buy a car.

8. Julio rents the apartment he takes the bus to work.

Proofreader's Marks

Add text:

    Julio will take his time.
But
    he is ready to move.

Add a comma:

    Julio will take his time

    but he is ready to move.

Do not capitalize:

    Julio will take his time,

    but He is ready to move.

See all Proofreader's Marks on page ix.

Write It

C. Complete each compound sentence about an apartment you would like to live in.

9. I would like to rent an apartment, but _____.

10. _____, and it would be close to my friend's house.

11. My apartment would be small, but _____.

12. _____, or I would have to borrow money from my parents.

D. (13–15) Write three compound sentences that tell how you would afford an apartment and how you would take care of it. Use **and**, **but**, and **or**.

_____

_____

_____

_____

_____

Edit It

E. (16–20) Edit the list of landlord's rules. Fix the mistakes in the compound sentences.

Rules for Your Apartment

You must sign a lease. I want your parents to co-sign it.
You may not have dogs, cats are okay.
You can pay your rent in cash you can pay me by check.
You can sublet your apartment. But I have to meet the new renter.
Garbage collection is on Tuesdays, You have to put your garbage out on the curb.
You can have friends visit. The noise level must be kept low.

Proofreader's Marks
Delete: I will move͡s but I don't know when.
Add text: and I found a place, I like it a lot.
Add a comma: I can move Friday or I can move Saturday.
Do not capitalize: The place is small, ~~B~~ut it seems big.

194

88 What's a Run-on Sentence?

A Sentence That Goes On and On

- To fix a run-on sentence, break it into shorter sentences.

  Run-On: Pedro wants a part-time job and he looks in the newspaper and he sees an ad for a job at the ice-cream store.

  Better: Pedro wants a part-time job. He looks in the newspaper, and he sees an ad for a job at the ice-cream store.

- Sometimes you can also rearrange words to express the same idea.

  Run-On: Pedro goes to the store and he fills out an application and the manager notices his experience and it is extensive.

  Better: Pedro goes to the store, and he fills out an application. The manager notices his extensive experience.

Try It

A. Edit these run-on sentences. Break them into shorter sentences.

1. The manager interviews Pedro and he tells her about his job last summer and it was in a restaurant and Pedro made the ice-cream desserts.

2. Pedro wants to work part-time because he is in school and the manager needs someone to work weekends and she needs someone to work one or two days after school, too.

3. That is perfect for Pedro and he tells the manager that he is interested in the job and the manager tells him that she is interviewing today and tomorrow and she will call him soon.

4. Pedro thanks her and goes home and he turns on his computer and looks for other jobs online and he sees one for a local restaurant and Pedro decides to apply there, too.

5. Pedro fills out an online application and then he waits a few days and he decides to call about both

Proofreader's Marks
Add a comma: Pedro works hard and   he is glad.
Add a period: He leaves early He   returns late.
Delete: He works. and He smiles.
Capitalize: He plays, too. he is   happy.
See all Proofreader's Marks   on page ix.

B. Rewrite each run-on sentence. Break it into shorter sentences and rearrange the words.

6. Pedro learns to make ice-cream cakes and the cakes are fun to design and Pedro enjoys designing them and the manager likes his designs and his designs are creative.

_____

_____

_____

7. Pedro works at his job all summer and then school starts and the ice-cream season is over and the store closes for the season and Pedro wants to work during the school year and he looks for a part-time job.

_____

_____

_____

Write It

C. What kind of job do you think Pedro will look for? Complete the sentences. Fix any run-ons.

8. Pedro looks for a job in a _____ because _____.

9. To look for a job, he _____.

10. He finds an ad for an interesting job, and he _____.

11. The manager _____.

D. (12–15) What kind of job would you like to have? How would you find your perfect job. Write at least four sentences. Then reread your sentences and fix run-ons.

_____

_____

_____

_____

89 How Do You Fix a Run-on Sentence?

Break It Into Shorter Sentences.

- Some run-on sentences include too many phrases or clauses divided by **commas**.

   Yesterday my family ran out of fruit, cheese, and milk, and we needed them for dinner, and I offered to go to the grocery store, and buy the groceries, and I couldn't believe how expensive it was to buy just fruit, cheese, and milk.

- To fix run-ons, create shorter, more understandable sentences.

   Yesterday my family ran out of fruit, cheese, and milk, and we needed them for dinner. I offered to go to the grocery store and buy the groceries. I couldn't believe how expensive it was to buy just fruit, cheese, and milk.

Try It

A. Edit these run-on sentences. Break them into shorter sentences.

1. Groceries are expensive, but they are necessary, and my family needs to grocery shop every week, and sometimes we run out of bread, orange juice, or milk, and need to shop more often.

2. Mom and Dad make a budget, and they budget a certain amount for the groceries, and they budget extra money on special occasions like birthdays, anniversaries, or holidays.

3. Sometimes we have a lot of food leftover from dinner, and we have leftovers the next night, and my favorite leftover dinners are chicken pot pie, beef stew, and enchiladas.

4. Mom and Dad budget their grocery money well, and we sometimes have money left over, and we can go out to breakfast, lunch, or dinner, and I like going out to dinner the best.

5. I'm learning about budgeting money, and I will live on my own one day, and I will know how to budget my own money, and I will stick to my budget, and be able to afford the things I want!

Proofreader's Marks
Add a period: I like lemons. She likes limes.
Delete: They sell fruit but and vegetables.
Capitalize: He likes cheese. he likes it cold.
See all Proofreader's Marks on page ix.

B. Rewrite each run-on sentence. Break it into shorter sentences.

6. Kara just moved into her first apartment, and she needs groceries, dishes, and silverware, and first she goes to the grocery store, and the groceries are very expensive, and Kara decides she will have to budget her money.

_____

_____

_____

7. Kara gets home, sits down, and figures out a budget, and every week she sticks to her budget, and soon she saves some extra money, and she treats herself to a special meal.

_____

_____

_____

Write It

C. Complete the sentences about budgeting for groceries. Fix any run-ons.

8. At the grocery store, I always want to buy _____ because _____
_____ .

9. Sometimes I don't have enough money, and I _____
_____ .

10. I have extra money, and I _____ .

11. Groceries are expensive, but _____
_____ .

D. (12–15) Write at least four sentences about budgeting your money. Fix any run-ons.

_____

_____

_____

_____

90 Use Compound Sentences

Remember: A compound sentence includes two independent clauses joined by **and**, **but**, or **or**.

- Use **and** to join like ideas. Use **but** to join different ideas. Use **or** to show a choice.

    Do you go to school, **or** do you have a full-time job? I go to school, **and** I think that I have a busy life. My brother has a full-time job. Sometimes I envy him, **but** then I realize that he works hard all day. I'm glad I still have some free time!

- Don't overuse **and**.

    Students work hard at school, and adults work hard at work. and adults

    need to be responsible and ~~adults need to~~ earn money to pay bills.

Try It

A. Edit the sentences. Use and, but, or or to make each pair of sentences into a compound sentence.

1. Working adults are independent. They have a lot of responsibilities.

2. Both of my parents work. They make money to support our family.

3. Would you rather be working full time? Are you glad you are a student?

B. Edit these run-on sentences. Break them into shorter sentences.

4. Matt dropped out of school and he is working now and he has to pay his own bills and he can't waste his money.

5. Matt wants to get a GED and he is going to school at night and he studies hard and he is always busy and he is always tired.

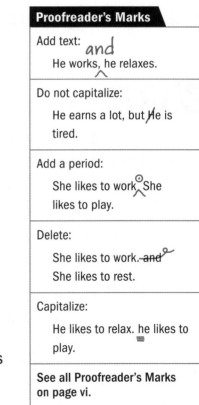

Proofreader's Marks

Add text: and
He works, he relaxes.
                          ∧

Do not capitalize:
He earns a lot, but ̸He is tired.

Add a period:
She likes to work⊙ She likes to play.

Delete:
She likes to work. ~~and~~
She likes to rest.

Capitalize:
He likes to relax. he likes to play.

See all Proofreader's Marks on page vi.

Write It

C. Write compound sentences to answer the questions. Use **and**, **but**, and **or**.

6. How much free time do you have on weekdays and on weekends? _____

_____

7. How do you manage your time? _____

_____

8. What choices do you make when you manage your time? _____

_____

D. (9–12) Do you think it's easier to be an adult with a job or a teenager in high school? Write at least four compound sentences to explain your opinion. Fix any run-ons.

_____

_____

_____

_____

_____

Edit It

E. (13–15) Edit this conversation between two teens. Fix one run-on sentence. Create two compound sentences.

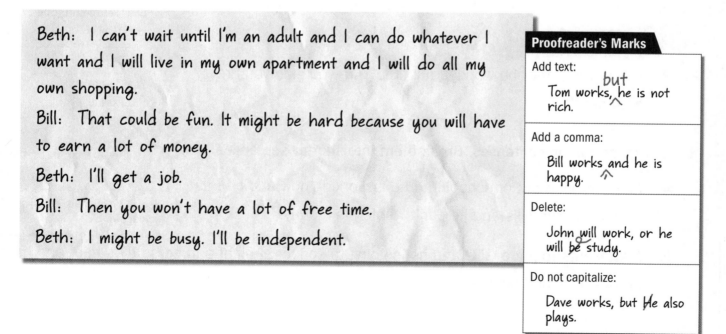

Beth: I can't wait until I'm an adult and I can do whatever I want and I will live in my own apartment and I will do all my own shopping.

Bill: That could be fun. It might be hard because you will have to earn a lot of money.

Beth: I'll get a job.

Bill: Then you won't have a lot of free time.

Beth: I might be busy. I'll be independent.

Proofreader's Marks

Add text:

Tom works, ^but he is not rich.

Add a comma:

Bill works ^and he is happy.

Delete:

John will work, or he will be~~ study~~.

Do not capitalize:

Dave works, but /He also plays.

Edit and
Proofread

✓ Capitalize the Titles of Publications

- Capitalize all main words in the titles of books, magazines, newspapers, and articles.

    Book: *Cell Phone Culture*

    Magazine: *Consumer Reports*

    Newspaper: *USA Today*

    Article: "Best Cell Phone Deals"

- Do not capitalize small words such as **a, an, the,** and **of** unless they are the first word in the title.

    "Acquiring Wireless Equipment and Service"

    The Cell Phone Handbook

Try It

A. (1–10) Fix ten capitalization errors in the paragraph. Use proofreader's marks.

I read an interesting article in teen vogue about teens and cell phones. It was titled "Call waiting." The article talked about teen cell phone use. It quoted an article from the Los Angeles times in which scientists said that cell phones could affect the way our brains are wired. It also mentioned the article "Restriction On The Use Of Cell Phones While Driving" by the Harvard Center for Risk Analysis. At the end, the article quoted etiquette expert Jacqueline Whitmore, who has published articles in the wall street journal.

Proofreader's Marks

Capitalize:

I like to read TV guide.

Do not capitalize:

Have you ever read
Car And Driver?

See all Proofreader's Marks
on page ix.

B. Answer each question. Be sure to capitalize titles correctly.

11. What is the name of your school newspaper?

_____

12. What is the last book you read?

_____

✓ Use Italics and Underlining

- Use italics (in a word processing program) or underlining (when writing by hand) for the titles of works that are not part of another larger work. For example, titles of:
  - books
  - magazines and journals
  - newspapers
  - movies and plays
  - TV and radio programs
  - paintings and sculptures

  Kaitlyn is reading *Popular Mechanics*.
  Have you seen the movie <u>Cellular</u>?

- Use quotation marks with the titles of works that are part of a larger work. For example, titles of:
  - poems
  - short stories
  - articles
  - chapters

  Please read the chapter "Twentieth Century Inventions" in your textbook.
  I love the poem "The Telephone" by Robert Frost.

Try It

A. (13–16) Fix four errors with italics or underlining. Use proofreader's marks.

When I got to school the other morning, I realized that I'd left The American Short Story, my English textbook, at home. I needed it because I had to give a presentation in class on the story <u>The Gift of the Magi</u>. Luckily, I was able to call my mom on my cell phone, and she brought the book to school. In the afternoon, I realized I'd also forgotten my script for The Crucible, our spring play. I had to call my mom again, and she wasn't happy about it. For my birthday, she bought me a copy of the book How to Be Organized in Spite of Yourself. I got the message.

Proofreader's Marks

Add underlining:

No, I was reading the book <u>To Kill a Mockingbird</u>.

Add quotation marks:

I also read the story "The Tell-Tale Heart."

Delete:

I read the chapter "Making Lists."

✔ Check Your Spelling

When adding a suffix that begins with a vowel, such as **-ing**, **-ed**, **-en**, **-er**, or **-y**, to certain words, you need to double the final consonant of the word.

Double the final consonant when:

- the word has only **one syllable** and ends in a single consonant (other than **w**, **x**, **y**, or **z**).

One-syllable Word	Suffix	New Word
shop	**-er**	shopp**er**
wit	**-y**	witt**y**

- the word has **more than one syllable** and the stress is on the final syllable.

Multisyllable Word	Suffix	New Word
unplug	**-ing**	unplugg**ing**
prefer	**-ed**	preferr**ed**

Try It

A. Complete each sentence by adding the appropriate suffix to the word in parentheses.

17. Last month, our school _____ cell phones. **(ban)**

18. Students had to stop _____ with their friends via text messaging. **(chat)**

19. The teachers, however, _____ that they liked the rule. **(admit)**

B. (20–24) Edit the article. Fix five spelling errors. Use proofreader's marks.

City Bans Cell Phones While Driving

The city of Chesterfield has recently forbiden the use of cell phones while driving. People who disobey the law can be stoped by police and ticketed. The new law is spliting public opinion in half. Many residents think the law is a wining step towards public safety. Others think the government is begining to intrude in its citizens' lives.

Proofreader's Marks

Change text:
Are you si̶t̶i̶n̶g down?
sitting
∧

✓ Form Compound Sentences

Use a coordinating conjunction to join two related sentences.

Coordinating Conjunction	Meaning	Example
and	joins sentences with two similar ideas	Danny owns a cell phone, **and** he uses it all the time.
but	joins sentences with two contrasting ideas	Rosa has a cell phone, **but** she hardly ever uses it.
or	joins sentences with alternative ideas	Jada uses her cell phone, **or** she uses her home phone.

Be sure to place a comma before the conjunction in a compound sentence.

Try It

A. Combine each pair of sentences to make a compound sentence. Be sure to use the correct coordinating conjunction.

25. I want to get a cell phone plan. I don't know anything about them.

_____

26. You can choose a prepaid plan. You can choose a standard plan.

_____

27. You get free nighttime minutes. You get a new phone every two years.

_____

28. This phone can send text messages. It can also send picture messages.

_____

29. I'll get that phone. Can I get it in red?

_____

30. It comes in black. It comes in silver.

_____

91 What's a Complex Sentence?

A Sentence with Two Kinds of Clauses

- A clause has a **subject** and a **verb**. An **independent clause** can stand alone as a sentence.

    My **friends like** to be part of school activities.
    <u>independent clause</u>

- A **dependent clause** also has a subject and a verb, but it cannot stand alone.

    because they like to be noticed
    <u>dependent clause</u>

- You can "hook" the dependent clause to an independent clause to form a complete sentence. The new sentence is called a **complex sentence**.

    My friends like to be part of school activities **because they like** to be noticed.
    <u>independent clause</u>   <u>dependent clause</u>

Try It

A. Draw a line from an independent clause to a dependent clause to combine into a complex sentence.

1. I score goals	after Ann did.
2. Mara tried out for the play	when she finishes a painting.
3. Spike plays the drums	whenever Stella plays.
4. Nick goes to basketball games	because I like the cheers.
5. Kim sets up an art show	because he knows Kim likes music.
6. I exercise after school	when he goes to games.
7. Stella plays really hard	because I want to look good.
8. Nick wears his best clothes	when her parents are there.
9. Ann will get an award	after she writes her essay.

B. Use the words to make complex sentences. Punctuate your sentences correctly.

10. Stella / she wants to be team captain / because / works so hard _____

_____

11. after / Stella will get a trophy / the season is over _____

_____

12. Spike puts on his uniform / he marches in the parade / before _____

_____

13. Kim sets up shows / she wants artists to share their work / because _____

_____

14. Ann goes out with her friends / after / the play _____

_____

Write It

C. Answer the questions about yourself and what makes you an individual. Use complex sentences.

15. When you meet someone for the first time, what do you think they notice about you?

I think _____.

16. What do you do to impress people when you first meet them? When I first meet them,

I _____.

17. After you accomplish something, how do you feel? Explain why. After I _____

_____.

D. (18–20) Now write at least three sentences about how you are like other people you know and how you are different. Use complex sentences.

_____

_____

_____

_____

92 What's One Way to Create a Complex Sentence?

Use *Because* or *Since*.

- A **complex sentence** has one independent clause and one dependent clause.

    My brother never talks to me **when we are at school.**
    _____ independent clause _____   _____ dependent clause _____

- When a dependent clause acts like an adverb, it begins with a **subordinating conjunction**. It is called an adverb clause.

    Some subordinating conjunctions tell why.

    He rides his bike **because** he doesn't like the bus.

    Since he doesn't like the bus, he rides his bike.

Try It

A. Draw a line from an independent clause to a dependent clause to combine them into a complex sentence.

1. my brother can get himself to school.

   because he wants to meet new friends.

2. he spends more time alone at home.

   because I try not to bother him.

3. My brother is polite and friendly

   since he needs to have a laugh.

4. I try to make him laugh

   because he just walks away.

5. He hopes his new bike will impress people

   because our parents are strict about that.

6. he hasn't spent much time with me.

   Since his best friend moved away,

7. I don't ask him many questions

   Since he got his new bike,

8. I think he likes me

   Because he is two years older than me,

B. Choose words from each column to build four complex sentences. You can use words more than once.

My brother got a new bike He wants to win new friends My parents let him make some decisions They encourage him	since because	he wants to meet new people. they think he is old enough. they want him to have a goal. he misses his old friend.

9. _____

10. _____

11. _____

12. _____

Write It

C. Your best friend, brother, or sister is becoming independent. You miss the time you spent together. What do you do? Use complex sentences to explain.

13. When did your friend, brother, or sister start to change? _____

14. Why has he or she changed? _____

15. Is he or she changing to impress someone else? Why? _____

_____

16. Do you agree that the changes are an improvement? _____

_____

D. (17–20) Write at least four sentences to tell more about a friend, brother, or sister who has changed. Use complex sentences.

_____

_____

_____

_____

_____

93 What's Another Way to Create a Complex Sentence?

Use *When, After,* or *Before.*

> The subordinating conjunctions **when**, **after**, and **before** tell when an action happens. They can begin an **adverb clause**.
>
> - Use **when** if the action in the independent and dependent clauses happens at the same time.
>   Aunt Jill smiles **when** <u>she greets people in her neighborhood.</u>
>
> - Use **after** if the dependent clause tells what happens first.
>   **After** <u>she has breakfast,</u> she takes a walk.
>
> - Use **before** if the dependent clause tells what happens later.
>   Aunt Jill works at her studio **before** <u>she eats lunch.</u>

Try It

A. Write an adverb clause to complete each sentence. Use **when**, **after**, or **before**.

1. _____ Aunt Jill went to Italy to study art. **(after)**

2. She studied painting _____. **(when)**

3. _____ she also learned about fashion. **(when)**

4. She always likes to look her best _____. **(before)**

B. Use the conjunctions **when**, **after**, or **before** to combine each pair of sentences.

5. Aunt Jill puts on beautiful clothes. She goes out to dinner.

_____

6. She finishes her dinner. She stays out late dancing.

_____

7. In the early morning she has coffee. She starts work.

_____

Write It

C. Answer the questions about yourself and traits that you admire. Use complex sentences.

8. Write about a time an adult made a favorable impression on you. _____

_____

9. What are the things you admired about this person? _____

_____

10. Would this person be a good role model? _____

_____

D. (11–14) Write at least four sentences to tell more about an aunt, uncle, teacher, or other adult whom you admire. Use complex sentences.

_____

_____

_____

_____

Edit It

E. (15–20) Edit the journal entry. Use conjunctions and proofreader's marks to form six complex sentences.

August 8

Before the summer is over, I want to make some plans. I want to study art. I finish high school. I can travel. I earn enough money. I need to get good grades. I apply to colleges. I want to learn about fashion, too. I go to Italy. I want to be like Aunt Jill. I grow up. I want to be friendly and interesting like she is. I am older.

> **Proofreader's Marks**
>
> Change text:
> I have to earn money ^before^ I can travel.
>
> See all Proofreader's Marks on page ix.

94 What's Another Way to Create a Complex Sentence?

Use *Although* or *Unless*.

A dependent clause that begins with **although** or **unless** acts like an adverb. These subordinating conjunctions in the adverb clauses have different meanings.

- Use **although** to make a contrast between two events.

  Although I could not be with my friends, I enjoyed what I was doing.

- Use **unless** to tell about a condition.

  My friend Ben said he would be upset **unless** I could join them.

Try It

A. Write an adverb clause to complete each sentence. Use **although** or **unless**.

1. _____ I enjoy my work at the shelter. **(although)**

2. My friends are upset _____. **(unless)**

3. _____ I really like the shelter, too. **(although)**

4. My friends think I will not improve at basketball _____. **(unless)**

B. Draw a line to an adverb clause to make a complete sentence.

5. I like to work at the homeless shelter,   although he misses spending time with me.

6. The homeless people would get sad   although I also like to see my friends.

7. Now, Ben likes what I do,   unless I showed up.

8. my friends were upset at first.   Although they understand now,

C. Imagine your friends are upset because you can't spend time with them on Saturdays. You help an elderly neighbor that day. Answer the questions. Use complex sentences.

9. What do you tell your friends about your Saturdays? _____

10. What might your friends think about you? _____

11. How do you try to help them understand you? _____

12. What choice are you making about what is important to you? _____

_____

D. (13–16) Now write at least four sentences to tell more about what is important to you. Use **although** and **unless**.

_____

_____

_____

_____

Edit It

E. (17–20) Edit the journal entry. Fix four mistakes with conjunctions.

October 10

I try to be polite, although many people are not. whenever I do not do it for attention, I think other people notice this about me. My younger cousin isn't always polite when I remind him. because I think it doesn't make a difference anymore, I will continue to be polite. because other people are not always polite, that doesn't mean I should stop.

Proofreader's Marks

Change text:

We wanted to help out, ~~when~~ although there were enough people.

See all Proofreader's Marks on page ix.

95 Use Complex Sentences

Remember: Varied sentences make writing interesting. One way to create variety is to use adverb clauses to make complex sentences.

- Tell why by adding an adverb clause with **because** or **since**.
  Because I want to fit in, I dress nicely.

- Tell when by adding an adverb clause with **when**, **after**, or **before**.
  I want to make a good impression **when** I meet a new group of kids.

- Make a contrast by adding an adverb clause with **although**. Tell about a condition by adding an adverb clause with **unless**.
  Although I am late, I stop to talk with my mom.
  She doesn't like me to go out **unless** she knows where I am going.

Try It

A. Write an adverb clause to complete each sentence. Use the subordinating conjunction in parentheses.

1. I was so excited about this party _____. (when)

2. I am a little nervous _____. (because)

3. _____, I know it's more important to be myself. (Although)

B. Write the words in the correct order to make complex sentences. Punctuate your sentences correctly.

4. the party was over / I learned that people liked me / after _____

   _____

5. because / someone said I was nice / I listened well _____

   _____

6. I won't be as nervous next time / although / I was nervous last time _____

   _____

C. Answer the questions about yourself and meeting new people. Use adverb
clauses in your sentences.

7. How do you feel when you meet new people? When I meet new people, I _____

_____.

8. What do you want your actions and words to say about you? I want _____

_____.

9. How do the actions and words of other people affect your impression of them? _____

_____

D. (10–14) Now write at least four sentences with adverb clauses. Tell more
about how you try to be yourself in new situations.

_____

_____

_____

_____

Edit It

E. (15–20) Improve the journal entry. Use conjunctions correctly.

April 15

I try to be a good listener when I meet people.
whenever I listen, I also try not to be too quiet.
People like it when you talk about yourself,
before you talk too much. It is important to
be polite, nobody likes a person who is rude.
because the party, I tell myself some jokes.
After I am usually nervous, the jokes help me
relax. When the party, I have some new friends!

Proofreader's Marks

Add a word:
                    when
I laugh ^ I am really
nervous.

Change text:
                    when
I laugh ~~after~~ I am really
nervous.

See all Proofreader's Marks
on page ix.

96 Why Do Verbs Have So Many Forms?

Because They Change to Show When an Action Happens

The tense of a verb shows when an action happens.

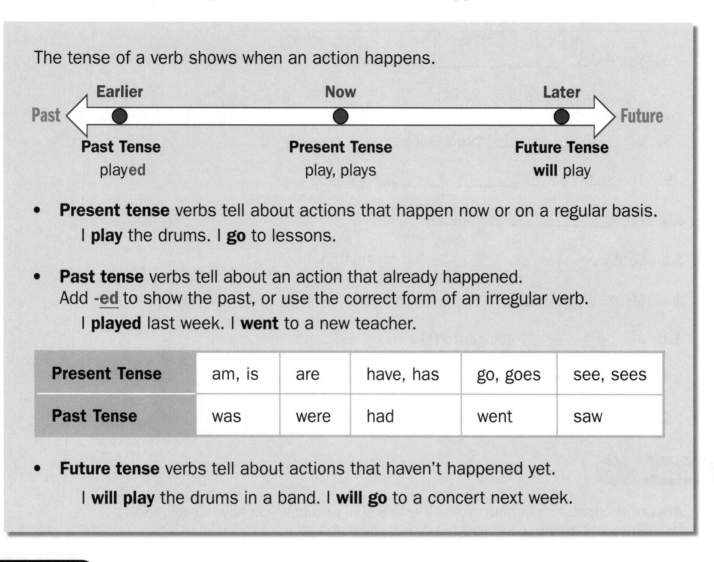

- **Present tense** verbs tell about actions that happen now or on a regular basis.

  I **play** the drums. I **go** to lessons.

- **Past tense** verbs tell about an action that already happened.
  Add **-ed** to show the past, or use the correct form of an irregular verb.

  I **played** last week. I **went** to a new teacher.

Present Tense	am, is	are	have, has	go, goes	see, sees
Past Tense	was	were	had	went	saw

- **Future tense** verbs tell about actions that haven't happened yet.

  I **will play** the drums in a band. I **will go** to a concert next week.

Try It

A. Write the past tense form of the verb in parentheses.

1. Last year, I _____ how to play the drums. **(learn)**

2. My teacher _____ me how to hold the sticks. **(show)**

3. When I started, I _____ very nervous. **(is)**

4. I _____ no idea how I would play. **(have)**

5. After the first lesson, I _____ a solo on the drums. **(play)**

B. Complete each sentence with a verb from the box. Use the correct tense of the verb: present, past, or future. You can use words more than once.

is	join	like	practice	want	are	work

6. Yesterday, I _____ a garage band.

7. The members always say they _____ how I play.

8. We _____ three times a week now.

9. The guitar player _____ very good.

10. I _____ to improve.

11. Last week, I _____ on my rhythm.

12. My parents _____ surprised when they heard me play.

13. I _____ eager to take more lessons.

14. Tomorrow, the band _____ on a new song.

15. I _____ very excited to help write the music.

Write It

C. Answer the questions about yourself and a skill or talent you have developed. Use sentences to show present, past, or future tenses.

16. What skill or talent are you most proud of? I *can* _____.

17. When do you first discover your skill or talent? I *discovered it when* _____
_____.

18. Has this skill or talent increased your confidence? I _____.

D. (19–20) Now write at least two sentences to tell more about yourself and a talent or skill that you have developed.

_____

_____

_____

_____

97 What If An Action Happened But You're Not Sure When?

Use the Present Perfect Tense to Tell About It.

- If you know when an action happened in the past, use a **past tense** verb.

   Last month, Tony and Ben **cared** for the dogs.

- If you're not sure when a past action happened, use a verb in the **present perfect tense**.

   They **have cared** for the dogs many times.

- To form the present perfect, use the helping verb **have** or **has** plus the **past participle** of the main verb. For regular verbs, the past participle ends in **-ed**.

Verb	Past Tense	Past Participle
care	cared	cared
beg	begged	begged
cry	cried	cried

Try It

A. Complete each sentence. Use the past tense or the present perfect tense.

1. Last year, Tony _____ take care of his neighbor's dogs.
   helped / has helped

2. Ben also _____ for dogs many times to earn extra money.
   cared / has cared

3. Last month, Tony and Ben _____ to work together.
   decided / have decided

4. They _____ their own business.
   started / have started

5. Yesterday, Ben _____ feed the dogs.
   helped / has helped

6. Tony _____ with the dogs many times before.
   played / has played

B. Write the correct past tense or present perfect tense of the verb in parentheses.

7. They _____ their business tasks. **(organize)**

8. Last week, Ben _____ the dogs. **(wash)**

9. Tony _____ neighbors if they need dog-walkers. **(ask)**

10. Yesterday, they _____ to buy dog treats. **(decide)**

11. They _____ all of the dogs they are watching. **(like)**

12. The neighbors _____ a bill for the work. **(receive)**

13. Last week, Tony _____ the money. **(collect)**

14. Then, they _____ the money from the business. **(divide)**

15. Tony and Ben _____ the money to build the business. **(use)**

Write It

C. Answer the questions about yourself and a business idea you have. Use past tense and present perfect tense in your sentences.

16. What have you created as part of a hobby or activity? I _____
_____.

17. In the past two years, have you earned money for something you can do or make? In the past two years, I _____
_____.

18. What have you noticed about small businesses in your neighborhood? I _____
_____.

D. (19–20) Write at least two sentences to tell more about how you can use what you know to start a small business. Use past tense and present perfect tense verbs.

_____
_____
_____

98 What If a Past Action Is Still Going On?

Then Use the Present Perfect Tense.

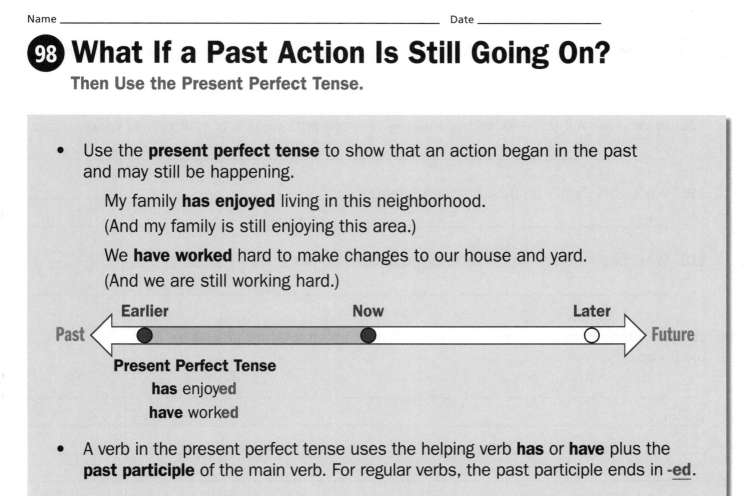

- Use the **present perfect tense** to show that an action began in the past and may still be happening.

    My family **has enjoyed** living in this neighborhood.
    (And my family is still enjoying this area.)

    We **have worked** hard to make changes to our house and yard.
    (And we are still working hard.)

    Past ◄──●──────────●──────────○──► **Future**
    Earlier   Now   Later

    Present Perfect Tense
      has enjoy**ed**
      have work**ed**

- A verb in the present perfect tense uses the helping verb **has** or **have** plus the **past participle** of the main verb. For regular verbs, the past participle ends in **-ed**.

Try It

A. Complete each sentence by writing the present perfect form of the verb in parentheses.

   1. My family _____ our house and yard. **(improve)**

   2. My mom _____ flowers and trees. **(plant)**

   3. My dad and I _____ the roof. **(fix)**

   4. We _____ a plan for the backyard. **(design)**

B. Rewrite each sentence to tell about something that began in the past. Use the present perfect tense.

   5. Maria and I follow the design plan. _____

   6. We create flower beds on both sides. _____

   7. We do not change the design. _____

C. Answer the questions about a project that you and your family are proud of.

8. What have you done to help your family improve or take care of your home? I have _____

_____.

9. What have family members done to help? _____

_____

10. What project has your family decided to work on next? We _____

_____.

D. (11–14) Write at least four sentences to tell more about a family project for the home.

_____

_____

_____

_____

_____

Edit It

E. (15–20) Edit the letter below. Fix six mistakes. Use the present perfect tense of the verbs.

Dear Rocco,

   My sister, Maria, and I have worked on the garden a lot lately. We follow a design plan. Maria have enjoyed filling the flower boxes. Dad and I move plants to the shady area. We finish most of the work already. Mom worked on it, too. Our neighbors enjoy our garden. We can't wait for you to see it!

Your friend,

Tabitha

Proofreader's Marks

Add text:
                have
We ∧ watered the garden.

Change text:
     have
I ~~has~~ helped my father.
  ∧

See all Proofreader's Marks on page ix.

99 Do All Past Participles End in *-ed*?

No, Irregular Verbs Have Special Forms.

- Past participles of most irregular verbs have a completely new spelling.

	Verb	Past Tense	Past Participle
Forms of *Be*	am, is	was	been
	are	were	been
	give	gave	given
	go	went	gone
	see	saw	seen

- Use **have** or **has** plus the past participle to form the **present perfect tense**.

  I **have been** in a new club this year. Sam **has been** part of this club, too.

Try It

A. Complete each sentence. Write the present perfect form of the verb in parentheses.

1. Our Nature Club _____ on many trips. **(go)**

2. We _____ canoeing. **(go)**

3. I _____ rock climbing. **(be)**

4. A forest guide _____ us lessons. **(give)**

B. (5–8) Add an irregular verb in the present perfect form to complete each sentence.

Sam, Nursal, and I _____ great friends for a long time. Nursal

_____ canoeing with us. We _____ the beauty of nature.

This group _____ all of us confidence.

C. Answer the questions about yourself and one way you have changed over the past school year. Use irregular verbs in present perfect tense in your sentences.

9. Do you think you are different in some way from a year ago? Why? I _____

_____.

10. How have you improved something about yourself? _____

_____

11. Were you inspired by someone who helped you change? _____

_____

D. (12–16) Now write at least five sentences to tell more about yourself and what has inspired change in you.

_____

_____

_____

_____

_____

_____

Edit It

E. (17–20) Edit the journal entry. Fix four mistakes.

June 25

We have returned from our trip. I be really happy in this group. I has tried new things because I feel comfortable with the group. I have went to so many new places. Since I am more confident, I have gave my friends information about joining this new group.

Proofreader's Marks

Change text:
seen
I have ~~see~~ wildlife.

See all Proofreader's Marks on page ix.

🄑 Verbs in the Present Perfect Tense

Remember: Use **have** or **has** plus the past participle of a verb to form the present perfect tense.

- The past participle of a **regular verb** ends in **-ed**.
  Uncle Derek **has helped** me with basketball. **(help + -ed)**
  I **have prepared** for the games with him. **(prepare [– e] + -ed)**

- The past participle of an **irregular verb** often has a completely new spelling.

Verb	Past Participle
be	been
come	come
get	got or gotten

Verb	Past Participle
hold	held
show	shown
take	taken

Try It

A. Write the correct form of the irregular verb to complete each sentence.
Use the present perfect tense.

1. Uncle Derek _____ a mini-camp to help basketball players. **(hold)**

2. I _____ at the court many times. **(be)**

3. Uncle Derek _____ me good tips for defense. **(show)**

4. We _____ all afternoon to review a new skill. **(take)**

5. Uncle Derek _____ to all of my games. **(come)**

6. He _____ many players to improve. **(get)**

7. Uncle Derek _____ me to some professional games. **(take)**

8. We _____ inspired by those athletes. **(be)**

B. Choose words from each column to build six sentences about gaining confidence. You can use words more than once.

I Uncle Derek My teammates	have been has been has given have gotten have taken	me praise. patient with me. assertive on the court. much better. lessons from him, too. very confident on the court.

9. _____

10. _____

11. _____

12. _____

13. _____

14. _____

Write It

C. Answer the questions about yourself and building confidence. Use the present perfect tense.

15. How have you felt when you do something well? I have felt _____.

16. Who has helped you to improve a skill or an ability? _____

17. How has this person helped you to improve? _____

D. (18–20) Now write at least three sentences to tell about what has made you feel confident about your abilities. Explain why.

_____

_____

_____

_____

_____

101 How Can I Fix a Fragment?

Add a Subject or a Predicate.

- A sentence is not complete unless it contains a subject and a predicate. If it does not have both, it is a **fragment**.

    In college, Julia.

    During the summer, she.

- To fix a fragment, add the missing part. What was added to make each fragment complete?

    In college, Julia **marched across the state**.

    During the summer, she **wrote letters to lawmakers**.

- Watch out for fragments in compound sentences, too. Remember that each clause needs a subject and a predicate. What was added to make this fragment complete?

    Fragment: The students for miles, and the people cheered.

    Sentence: The students **walked** for miles, and the people cheered.

Try It

A. (1–5) Add words to turn each fragment into a complete sentence.

   Julia is interested in fighting pollution. She was inspired by _____ in school. She _____ a march. She _____ to help the environment. She got _____ to join the march, too. _____ wore special T-shirts in the march.

B. Draw a line from each subject to the correct predicate.

   6. By the end of the march, Julia   praised Julia.

   7. With her great voice, Julia   were being a great listener and speaker.

   8. People in each town   was a leader.

   9. Her best traits   got people to listen to her.

   10. In every town, people   joined the march.

C. Complete the questions about someone who is unforgettable. Use a subject and predicate in your sentences.

11. Name at least two things this person does to get noticed. _____

_____

12. How do other people behave around this person? _____

_____

13. What special traits or talents does this person have? _____

_____

14. Why do people admire this person? _____

D. (15–17) Now write at least three sentences to tell about someone who has had a positive effect on you and why.

_____

_____

_____

_____

_____

Edit It

E. (18–20) Edit the flier. Fix three fragments.

We want you to join our march. We your help to stop pollution!

We are here to tell you about pollution in our state, and we your help!

We are asking you to sign this petition, and we want you to our march!

Proofreader's Marks
Add text:
will demand We ∧ new laws.
See all Proofreader's Marks on page ix.

102 How Else Can I Fix a Fragment?

Combine It With a Neighboring Sentence.

- If a fragment is a phrase, you often can fix it by combining it with a neighboring sentence. The result might be a compound sentence.

  Fragment: I admire Frankie. Am not alone.

  Sentence: I admire Frankie, and I am not alone.

  Fragment: Frankie no legs. He was not born that way.

  Sentence: Frankie has no legs, but he was not born that way.

- If a fragment is a dependent clause, you often can fix it by combining it with a neighboring sentence. The result might be a complex sentence.

  Fragment: Frankie was in an accident. When he was ten years old.

  Sentence: Frankie was in an accident when he was ten years old.

  Fragment: After the accident. He had to use a wheelchair.

  Sentence: After the accident, he had to use a wheelchair.

Try It

A. Read each sentence. Combine the sentences to fix the fragments. Edit each item to make a compound or complex sentence.

Proofreader's Marks

Change text:
We laugh. Have fun together. ,and we

Do not capitalize:
He Followed his dream.

See all Proofreader's Marks on page ix.

1. Frankie could not walk. Wanted to learn to use a wheelchair.

2. Julio taught Frankie. Learned fast.

3. He wanted to be an athlete. Didn't want the wheelchair to get in the way of his dream.

4. was in a race. Won first place.

5. When I watch Frankie. Can't believe what he can do.

6. Frankie lifts weights. Exercises every day.

7. I have never met anyone like him. My hero.

B. Fix the fragments. Write a complex or compound sentence.

8. Frankie has strong arms. Can move his wheelchair in any direction.

_____

9. He has no fear. When he is competing in a race.

_____

10. After each school day. He goes to the gym which is far away.

_____

11. He checks his wheelchair. Functions properly.

_____

12. Coach Jenner is patient. Pushes Frankie to improve his ability.

_____

13. Frankie worked very hard to master his wheelchair. Fine athlete.

_____

Write It

C. Answer the questions about someone you know who has had to overcome a physical handicap or other challenge. Fix fragments by combining sentences.

14. Who do you know who has overcome a physical handicap or special challenge? I _____

_____.

15. What do you admire about this person? Give two characteristics. I _admire_ _____

_____.

16. What have you learned from this person? I _have learned_ _____

_____.

D. (17–20) Write at least four sentences to tell more about what you can learn from someone with a physical handicap or other challenge.

_____

_____

_____

_____

228

103 How Can I Fix a Run-on Sentence?

Break It Into Two Sentences.

A **run-on sentence** is a very long sentence. You can fix a run-on sentence by breaking it into two compound sentences or a simple sentence and a compound sentence. (You may need to change some words.)

Run On: Christina sings in the shower **and** she sings on the bus **and** on the weekends she learns everything she can about music **and** she studies with a voice teacher.

Better: Christina sings in the shower, and she sings on the bus. On the weekends, she learns everything she can about music, and she studies with a voice teacher.

Better: Christina sings in the shower and on the bus. On the weekends, she learns everything she can about music and studies with a voice teacher.

Try It

A. Fix each run-on sentence. Edit each item to make two compound sentences or a simple sentence and a compound sentence.

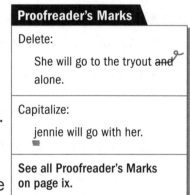

Proofreader's Marks

Delete:
    She will go to the tryout and
    alone.

Capitalize:
    jennie will go with her.

See all Proofreader's Marks on page ix.

1. Christina wants to be famous and be a star. and in our city, she wants to compete in the talent contest for a TV reality show.

2. In a week, she will go to tryouts and she will sing three songs. and she hopes she can sing well that day and she wants to make it to the next round of tryouts.

3. If she makes it to the final round, she will go to New York City and she will compete on TV. and she will wear a special outfit and people will help her fix her hair.

4. Christina wants to write her own music, and she wants to work with other musicians. and if she gets a record deal, and she will travel around the world.

5. Christina wants Selma to go with her to the tryout in our city and she wants Selma to go to the tryout in New York City. and she is planning to tell us everything and when they get back.

B. Rewrite each sentence to fix each run-on.

6. Christina rehearses with her teacher during the day and at night she listens to music and she writes songs. _____

_____

7. She has written fifteen songs and she is looking for musicians to work with her but it is hard to find good musicians. _____

_____

8. Christina and her mother are making the dress and she will wear it for the tryout and she will look beautiful. _____

_____

9. At first, Christina wanted to buy a dress for the competition but it costs too much money and she didn't have enough money. _____

_____

Write It

C. Answer the questions about a dream you have about your future. Use compound and complex sentences. Fix any run-on sentences.

10. What goals do you have for a career? | _____

_____.

11. How do you want to make a mark on the world? _____

_____

12. Who will support you in your goals? _____

_____

D. (13–15) Write at least three sentences to tell more about a goal or dream you have for your future. Use compound and complex sentences. Fix any run-on sentences.

_____

_____

_____

_____

Name _____ Date _____

104 How Can I Expand Sentences?

Try Adding Clauses.

There are many ways to make your writing more informative and more interesting. One way is to add clauses to sentences.

- You can add an independent clause (main clause) to create a compound sentence.

    Original: Anna laughs on camera.

    Expanded: Anna laughs on camera, and she talks about the fun times in the past.

- You can add a dependent clause to create a complex sentence.

    Original: I film my friends.

    Expanded: I film my friends because I know our lives will change soon.

Try It

A. Expand each sentence about recording an experience on film. Add the kind of clause named in parentheses.

1. I have been recording good times with my friends. **(dependent)**

_____

2. I want to make a record of our friendships. **(independent)**

_____

3. Benicio will edit the recordings. **(independent)** _____

_____

B. Write an independent or dependent clause to expand these sentences.

4. I have about 20 tapes recorded from the year, _____.

5. I will give the tapes to Benicio _____.

6. Everybody changed in a way _____.

7. The movie will be something we can share _____.

C. Answer the questions about one way that you record the events of your friendships. Expand your sentences to include compound and complex sentences.

8. Have you ever taken pictures or made video recordings of your friends? Why? I _____

_____

_____.

9. Have you shared any photos or recordings with friends? I _____

_____

_____.

10. What do your friends think of your work? They _____

_____

_____.

D. (11–12) Now write at least two sentences to tell more about how you record experiences with your friends. Use compound and complex sentences.

_____

_____

_____

_____

Edit It

E. (13–15) Edit the journal entry to expand the sentences. Add three independent or dependent clauses.

May 20

I use my video camera during the year.

My friend Benicio likes to tell jokes,

Anna dances

We will watch it together

Proofreader's Marks

Add text: , and we will make fun of each other. We will laugh

See all Proofreader's Marks on page ix.

232 © National Geographic Learning, a part of Cengage Learning, Inc.

105 Use Compound and Complex Sentences

Remember: You can combine **fragments** with other sentences to make compound or complex sentences. You can break **run-on sentences** into simple and compound sentences.

Fragment:	When I finished the book. Was shocked by the story.
Better:	When I finished the book, I was shocked by the story.
Run On:	After I closed the book, I thought about the author's experiences and I thought about the hardships and I gave the book to my friend.
Better:	After I closed the book, I thought about the author's experiences and hardships. Then, I gave the book to my friend.

Try It

A. (1–5) Fix each fragment or run-on sentence. Edit each item to make a compound or complex sentence.

When I started reading. Trouble relating to the author's experiences. I didn't understand how the author could be so happy and how she could be so positive. and then, the author had a different tone in the middle of the book. She had so many family troubles and she had tragedies. and I understood that the author was very strong and I admired her.

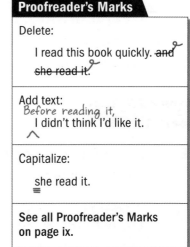

Proofreader's Marks

Delete:

I read this book quickly. ~~and she read it.~~

Add text:

Before reading it,
I didn't think I'd like it.

Capitalize:

she read it.

See all Proofreader's Marks
on page ix.

B. Read each fragment or run-on sentence. Make a compound or complex sentence. Write the new sentence.

6. The author moved to the United States from Africa. Told memorable stories. _____

_____

7. When I finished the book. I told everyone about this inspiring author. _____

_____

C. Answer the questions about an inspiring person you know or have read about. Use compound and complex sentences.

8. Who inspires you? I _____

_____ .

9. What makes this person unusual? _____

_____

10. What is the most memorable part of this person's story? _____

_____

D. (11–14) Now write at least four sentences to tell about an inspiring individual. Use compound and complex sentences.

_____

_____

_____

_____

Edit It

E. (15–20) Edit the postcard. Use proofreader's marks to fix fragments and make compound and complex sentences.

Dear Aunt Breanne,

Today I finished a great book, and I think you should read it. This athlete leaves Africa and arrives in the United States with no money. With no family. She has a long journey. After leaving her home country. She struggles and works. Makes goals. And wins the championship for the U.S. team in the end. I was inspired by this story and it changed my life. Might change yours, too.

Love,

Marisa

Proofreader's Marks
Delete:
I read ~~this~~ this book.
Add text:
Before reading it, I didn't think I'd like it.
Do not capitalize:
She left Home.
Add a period:
I liked it⊙
Capitalize:
she read it.